Let My People Go

Let My People Go

The Life of
Robert A. Jaffray

A.W. Tozer

Christian Publications

CAMP HILL, PENNSYLVANIA

Christian Publications
3825 Hartzdale Drive, Camp Hill, PA 17011

The mark of **✝** *vibrant faith*

ISBN: 0-87509-427-9
LOC Catalog Card Number: 90-80076
© 1990 by Christian Publications
Printed in the United States of America

94 93 92 91 90   5 4 3 2

Cover illustration by Karl Foster

Contents

P r e f a c e

NEXT TO THE HOLY SCRIPTURES the greatest aid to the life of faith may be Christian biography. It is indeed notable that a large part of the Bible itself is given over to the life and labors of prophets, patriarchs and kings—who they were, what they did and said, how they prayed and toiled and suffered and how they triumphed at last. Sometimes this is given in brief outline—a quick candid shot and no more—but often there is much fullness of detail covering page after page of the Sacred Word.

These favored ones whose names appear on the roll of the spiritually great have been adopted by succeeding generations of pilgrims as guides and teachers in the holy way. We have all felt their presence. We have stood with Abraham as he shielded his eyes and peered down the centuries to see by faith the fulfillment of the promise. We have sat with David under the pale light of the stars as, accompanied by his homemade lyre, he tried out some verses that were later to become immortal. Who among us has not been made wiser and better by knowing Elijah or Daniel or Paul? And who has not thanked God that their story was written down for us to read?

Only the conviction that a reading public would receive immeasurable aid from an acquaintance with the subject of this story gave me the courage to attempt it. The preparation of a biography of a person like Robert Jaffray is no easy task.

To write the life of a stay-put local citizen who had been content to spend his life in one town or even one country would not have been too great an undertaking. One might visit the old homestead, photograph his birthplace, interview a few people who knew him well, and the rest would be easy. But a person like Jaffray is not captured so painlessly. To collect data on one who lived all over the world and would never stay put is a real job for anyone.

Robert A. Jaffray was a citizen of no single country. From his early manhood he moved about over the face of the world—not aimlessly, but with clear intelligent purpose. He was an explorer, a pioneer, and this accounts for the gaps that will be found in this or any story of his life. He lived in too many places too far from each other to allow a closely woven biography to be written. One could have journeyed half way around the world to see him, only to find that he had left the day before to visit some remote point in the Far East where some important gathering looked to him for guidance.

Jaffray was a Canadian by birth. Wherever he traveled, *home* to him always meant Canada. Of Canada he was ever proud, and he remained loyal to his country as long as he lived. But he had met Christ as Moses had met God at the burning bush, and he had been baptized into His Spirit, made to feel the impulses of His heart. After that, Christ's people were his people in a sense none other could be. For the lost tribes of the earth he felt a kinship such as Moses felt for the children of Israel. He felt them to be God's people, though held under the bondage of sin. In the same way they were Jaffray's own people, and he was called to set them free. He distinctly heard a Voice saying, "Say to Pharaoh: Let my people go!"

This feeling of kinship with the lost of the earth and the conviction that he had been commissioned to deliver them from bondage made Jaffray a prophet and a deliverer, as surely as Moses had been before him. It was not until his last and greatest adventure, when he entered the East Indies, that he stated this conviction in so many words, but it had always been in the back of his mind and in the bottom of his heart, and it gave him an air of command.

We may as well know at the outset that we have here no ethereal saint full of the gentler graces but too sweet and fragile for this rough world. Anything but that! Jaffray was a man of authority; his whole bearing bespoke it, and everyone who knew him felt it unmistakably. Toward the powers of darkness he took a stern, condemning attitude, and in the name of God he was always saying, "Let my people go!"

Such facts as I have I now present to interested readers. I am certain that the power and drive of this unusual man will be felt by all who read what is written here. It is possible that the very attempt to bring a life so long and a character so rich and varied into the narrow compass of a small book may serve to focus attention upon him and allow his voice to be heard again, that voice which has been temporarily silenced by death.

One word should be added concerning the treatment of the material before me. I have sought to capture the spirit of Jaffray, to present him as a real human being. For this reason I have not given too much care to dates nor to mere chronological sequence. I have not tried to write a history of Alliance missions in the Far East, but to write the story of a person, and a person is always greater than anything he or she has done. I believe the facts set forth here will be found to be accurate, but my aim has been to show the man above and beyond the facts. How well I have succeeded is for others to judge.

I wish here to acknowledge the courtesy of Christian Publications for permitting me to quote from *After Fifty Years* and *With Christ in Indo-China*. I am also indebted to G. Ricordi and Company for permission to use the poem, *Go Down Moses*.

To the large number of Mr. Jaffray's friends and coworkers who so patiently submitted to my long cross-examinations and answered so cheerfully my endless prying questions, I also express my sincere thanks.

A.W. Tozer
Chicago
May 1, 1947

Introduction

THEN THE LORD SAID TO MOSES, "Get up early in the morning, confront Pharaoh and say to him, 'This is what the Lord, the God of the Hebrews, says: Let my people go so that they may worship me.' " Exodus 9:13

> When Israel was in Egypt's land,
>   Let my people go!
> Oppressed so hard they could not stand,
>   Let my people go!
>
> Go down, Moses,
>   'Way down to Egypt's land,
> Tell ol' Pharaoh to let my people go!
>   —Negro spiritual

As God's people were held by Pharaoh in the bondage of Egypt, so God has His people in every known and unknown tribe of the earth, who are held in worse bondage than that of Egypt. God proposes in His plan of redemption to release a people for His name.

All human beings are God's creation and possession. Temporarily Satan has usurped authority and, through sin, holds the race in bondage. As God sent Moses to say over and over again to Pharaoh, "Let my people go!" so He has sent the Lord Jesus to save the world. He has commanded

5

us to be His ministers to the last race of people in the uttermost parts of the earth, saying in the name of the Lord Jesus, the Creator and only Savior, "Let my people go!" This is the gospel message of deliverance.

Our missionaries have been busily engaged . . . in this wonderful work, delivering captives from the bondage of Satan. It is not an easy task, because it is directly a matter of challenging our archenemy, the Pharaoh of the world, saying to him over and over, in the name of the Lord, "Let my people go!"

Our work is not to try to improve the social conditions of the people of Egypt, but to call them out of Egypt and into a new life. They will become new creatures in Christ Jesus, living transformed lives, speaking a new language—the language of Zion—and singing a new song, "Worthy is the Lamb who was slain!"

Robert A. Jaffray, *The Pioneer*

1

Heritage

WHEN THE RETURNS ARE IN, it may be discovered that, for its size, no country has given to the world such a galaxy of spiritual giants as has Scotland. Whatever the reason, the fact is there for all to see. Out of Scotland have come preachers, missionaries, Bible expositors and Christian educators in numbers far out of proportion to its total population. Wherever its people have ranged over the earth, they have usually carried with them Scotland's plain Protestant faith and severe religious code. While there have been many individual exceptions, I think it will be found that they have stayed, for the most part, on the side of the angels, and the blessing of God has followed them down to the third and fourth generations.

It is no wonder, then, that one of the greatest missionaries of modern times should have been a Scot just one generation removed. He still had all his Highland courage and all his inherited love for hardships. Lust for action was strong upon him.

His grandfather, William Jaffray, was born in Thomasland, Scotland, in 1790 and was married only after he was well on in middle life. He and his wife, Margaret Heugh, had been married just a year when the first baby arrived at the Skeoch Farm home. Every two years thereafter came another, until there were nine in all—two daughters and seven sons. Some were given good, approved and solid names such as Janet and William and Margaret. Others had plainer ones—John and James and Alexander. George and Thomas were thrown in to finish out the nine. They were all baptized, the records say, by Mr. Raeburn or Mr. Logan or Mr. Robert Frew, and their names were duly entered in the Sessions Book of the kirk.

Those were the days when large families were born and small families were reared, the infant mortality rate being what it was. But the nine Jaffrays survived and lived, at least some of them, to a very advanced age. They were farmers, mostly, as native to the soil as the heather that grew beneath their feet. With one exception, they stayed close to the familiar old places with musical names: Thomasland near Airth, Skeoch near Bannonckburn, Throsk, and Stirling on the River Forth that flows from Loch Lomond to the sea.

The exception was Robert, the father of the missionary R.A. Jaffray. A strain of adventure led him while still quite a lad to break home ties and cross the ocean to Canada. He was, to stay by the figures, 20 years old when he arrived in Toronto in 1852. The Canada of that day was still young and relatively undeveloped, but to young Jaffray this was all in its favor. It did not offer too much ready-made comfort, but it did present a challenge—it afforded a young fellow a chance to begin at the bottom and grow up with the country. Jaffray decided to stay and spent the next years getting used to the new world, measuring the task and learning the ways of business and finance. That he learned these things well many Canadians know even today.

Jaffray married late, as his father had done before him, but the marriage, when it finally came, was a success from a social standpoint. His bride was Sarah Bugg, daughter of Alderman Bugg of the city of Toronto. This afforded a bit of a social boost, but it did not aid in the struggle for financial independence. So Jaffray entered the business world, becoming junior partner in a grocery concern with a Mr. Smith, the house being known as Smith and Jaffray.

Five children were born to the Jaffrays over the next years, three girls and two boys, and the sturdy family names appeared again—William, Robert and Margaret as well as Annie and Elizabeth. Things looked bright for the Jaffray family. The children were growing and so was the business. Then one day Jaffray woke to find out that he still had the family, but the business had disappeared. A fire had swept away everything, leaving him not just destitute but $10,000 in debt.

Here for the first time the true mettle of the man was proved. Of Mr. Smith we hear nothing more, but of Mr. Jaffray we hear much more indeed. It took disaster to wake the Scot in him and bring

out his fighting spirit. A few years of sharp struggle followed, but he soon got on his feet again
and gained an interest in a number of business
enterprises. Before long he was able to pay off his
debts, and from there he went on to make a fortune in real estate.

When past middle life, Mr. Jaffray became interested in the Toronto *Globe*, one of the great dailies
in the Dominion, bought a controlling interest
and proceeded to take over the paper—lock, stock
and barrel. At a time in life when many men are
planning to retire, he was entering the most influ-
ential phase of his career. Soon he was one of
the best-known figures in Canada. The *Globe*, a
liberal newspaper, prospered under the vigorous
leadership of its new owner. Jaffray was its animating spirit. It is not too much to say that for a
great many years Jaffray *was* the *Globe*.

Shortly after he had taken over the *Globe*, his
lumber interests—through which he had made his
fortune—were caught in a business slump. For
the second time Jaffray had everything swept
from under him. Nothing remained but the *Globe*
and a heavy, insistent debt.

His reputation was such that he managed to
survive without relinquishing his hold upon the
newspaper. Though no longer young, he fought
like a man in his twenties. The *Globe* paid out.
His debts were paid off and when he died at 82 he
was able to leave behind a sizable amount to be
divided among his heirs.

During the last years of his life he became so

well and favorably known throughout the business and political world that he was, at the age of 74, appointed to the Senate by order of the Council of the Canadian Government. He was still Senator Jaffray at the time of his death.

It may help in some measure to explain R.A. Jaffray—as far as any merely human factors can explain him—to see how the elder Jaffray met one after another of the difficult situations that confronted him during his long and active life. He could make and lose a fortune as if it were merely one more item in the month's work. Inexperience, lack of education, age, debt—nothing seemed to stop him as long as his health remained. The casual manner of dealing with impossibilities reveals a trait that appears to have descended from father to son without losing anything in the process. In another field of action the son showed the same courage, the same dogged cheerfulness under opposition, the same inability to know when he was beaten.

2

Early Life

ROBERT ALEXANDER JAFFRAY was born December 16, 1873. The home in which he grew up was one where the solid virtues were rated above all else and practiced by every member of the family. But it was not a home united spiritually. Sarah Jaffray, the wife and mother, was an ardent Christian and a faithful member of the church, but her husband could not see the light. He possessed the hardy moral nature of his Scottish forbears, but of personal faith he appears to have had little. To the claims of Christ he could not or would not respond.

At one time, it must be admitted, he even leaned far to the left in matters of belief. For a short while he attended the gatherings of a little band of "atheists" that met in the city of Toronto to discuss the mysteries of unbelief and warm their hands at the chill fires of their religious doubts. Mr. Jaffray appeared once in a while at these meetings, but the Protestant tradition was too strong in him to allow him to become enthusiastic over mere negations. He was rather apologetic about his association with these people and occasionally spoke very critically of them. Even if he did not have enough faith to become a Christian, he had too much to be a successful unbeliever. The proddings of conscience that must have come often to a person of his religious heritage he escaped by hard work and absorption in business affairs.

While her husband attended to his worldly interests, Sarah cared for her growing family, giving them the best religious training of which she was capable and taking them to the house of God on Sundays. If the father would not, then the mother would, and did—this happened in many other families besides the Jaffrays.

The childhood of Rob Jaffray—the name by which he was known to his family to the end of his life—could not have been a happy one. He was an overly stout boy, suffering from heart disease and diabetes. His disabilities excluded him from all sports and every form of play that required physical effort. When his friends started to have a game on some vacant lot, if Rob went with them he would be seen trudging heavily along behind. And when the game was at its height and the rest were running and shouting in their fun, he could only stand by pensively watching.

To those who knew Jaffray only after he had become a world missionary, it may come as a surprise to learn that he never recovered from this dual affliction. To the end of his life he was plagued by a weak heart, and while his excessive heaviness disappeared after he entered manhood, he was never entirely free from diabetes. While he did receive some relief at times, he was always on a restricted diet. What this must have meant to him during the course of his life only he could know. The vital need for a careful diet would seem to make extensive travel impossible. Yet R.A. Jaffray traveled hundreds of thousands of miles under every possible condition—from longboats to luxury liners—and his food was prepared by a wide assortment of kitchens from world-famous hotels to dirty huts on the banks of the swift-flowing Sesajap or Boelongan.

The Jaffrays were members of the Gould Street Presbyterian Church, and there each week they listened to the inspired preaching of the saintly Dr. Kellogg, one of the greatest preachers of Toronto in his day. When Rob was still a boy, the Gould Street Church consolidated with another located on St. James Square and the larger group that resulted became known as the St. James Square Presbyterian Church.

In this fellowship Rob was reared and here, when he was about 16 years old, he was soundly converted. His conversion to Christ came about through the efforts of a Sunday school teacher, Miss Annie Gowan, who had come under the spell of the preaching of Dr. A.B. Simpson during his many visits to Toronto.

A few years after his conversion, Rob went to hear Dr. Simpson in person, and from that time on his future was assured. After listening to one of Simpson's impassioned addresses, he threw himself at the feet of Christ and surrendered his entire life to Him and His cause.

He immediately became active in his home church, but the vision of a whole world lost would not let him rest content with church work. The call of the masses was upon his heart now and the urge of the Spirit was within him. He was not too sure yet, but vaguely he sensed that the voice of the Lord was saying to him, "I have indeed seen the misery of my people and I have come down to rescue them. So now, go. I am sending you to Pharaoh, and you shall say to him, 'Let my people go.' "

3

The Call

YOUNG JAFFRAY WAS EDUCATED in the public schools of Toronto and upon graduation from high school entered the Preparation School of Upper Canada College. After finishing there he decided against further studies for the time being and took a position with the Canadian Life Insurance Company. He was then 20 years old, and at this time the important encounter with A.B. Simpson took place.

The call to Christian service grew upon him with the passing of time, becoming more insistent until at last he could resist it no more. He must become a missionary! However he reasoned within himself, however he sought to excuse himself before God, however earnestly he pleaded his few gifts and lack of preparation, the way of peace for him lay in obedience to his vision, and he knew it.

In New York City some years prior, A.B. Simpson had founded a school to train workers for his rapidly growing missionary society. It was not a pretentious school. It offered no degrees and its prestige was precisely zero. But it did have low entrance requirements and the tuition was small.

Besides these advantages, it had an excellent faculty composed of learned and deeply devout men brought together by some kind of miracle from several evangelical denominations. Rob did not ponder for long. He decided to enter the New York Missionary Training Institute as his first real step toward the mission field.

Now came the hardest part of the job. He must inform his father and secure his consent to the plan. Robert Jaffray senior was no longer a young man. He had come up the hard way, had tasted power and had become accustomed to command. And he had his own plans for his sons. Will, the elder, he had slated to succeed him as editor and publisher of the powerful Toronto *Globe*, and Rob would continue in the highly lucrative insurance business. He just had to close his eyes to see Rob as one of Canada's richest men and to see Will and the *Globe* as a mighty molding force in the political future of the country. That was the man's dream, and up to that point he had an uncanny way of making his dreams come true.

Then young Rob walked in and quietly announced that he had decided to become a missionary to China. The expected happened. There was a stormy scene as the two Jaffrays met in a contest of will. It was an unequal battle with the advantage lying altogether on the side of the older man. Age, paternal authority and the strong leverage of economic pressure—all were on his side, while Rob had only his vision, his crusader's zeal and his dogged determination to obey God rather than man.

There is a story to the effect that the elder Jaffray, after threatening young Rob with disinheritance if he persisted in his plan, finally had a will drawn up cutting his son off altogether from the family fortune. Will Jaffray, Rob's elder brother, who was familiar with the whole thing from the beginning, staunchly denies this story, and the correspondence that I have examined is of such a nature as to make it seem very improbable. Admittedly, this removes the flavor of martyrdom—a flavor we enjoy when someone else is serving as the martyr. Knowing the slashing downright nature of the elder Jaffray, though, we find it easy to believe that in the urgency of the debate, he may have been led by the heat of his spirit to at least hint at the possibility of disinheritance if his son refused to abandon his senseless and fanatical plan.

One fact that may have given rise to the disinheritance story was the elder Jaffray's flat refusal to finance Rob's schooling at the Missionary Training Institute. If he would consent to a compromise and enter the regular Presbyterian ministry in Canada, all would be well and good. His needs would be met from the family exchequer. But Simpson! China! Never! And that was that.

By the time September rolled around things had quieted down somewhat. Rob would go to New York and work his way through school. His father was somewhat reconciled, but certainly not convinced. No one could do anything with Rob in his present state of mind—that was evident. But things might change. He would wait and see. "If the Alliance sends you to China," he told his son, "they'll pay every penny of the expense. Not a dime will you get from me." Then softening a little, "But if you decide the whole thing was a mistake and want to come home, just let me know. I'll send you the money."

Now followed three years of hard study. The curriculum of that early missionary school boasted no fancy subjects. Those who entered its doors cared little about the liberal arts, nor were they much interested in technical subjects except as they had practical bearing upon the work of world missionaries. The minds of those first students were focused. They were there to gain the essential training that would enable them to preach the gospel in places where Christ had not yet been named and where they burned to go at the earliest possible moment.

4

The Missionary Imperative

ABOUT THIS TIME A MISSIONARY REVIVAL had begun to make itself felt here and there in the United States and Canada. A.B. Simpson was one of its leaders, partly the cause and partly the result of it. Under his inspiration the school—indeed the entire Alliance movement—flamed with missionary zeal. All human learning, all theology was directed to this one channel. The hope of Christ's return, which had spread among the churches with something like prairie-fire rapidity, gave added urgency to the missionary passion. This was especially true of the doctrine as Simpson interpreted it.

According to his view, the second coming was contingent upon world evangelization. Christ could not return until the gospel had been preached among all nations for a witness. The conclusion was plain. The Lord's return could actually be hastened by zealous missionary activity. One had a direct bearing upon the other. One theme ran through the preaching and writings of Simpson: Bring back the King. "Why say ye not a word about bringing back the King?'' was the re-proachful text often used in those days to arouse slumbering interest and to incite zeal for world evangelization. Though many learned eyebrows were raised at this interpretation, its practical effect upon its adherents was terrific. Nice exegesis and sober analysis would never want for advocates; mere Bible teaching could be done by others. Simpson and his Alliance refused to be satisfied with the dry bones of eschatology. In theology they were pragmatists. Their doctrines must work; they must result in practical activity in line with the purposes of God for this age. This is what they believed and what they taught. And their teaching had amazing power to catch and hold and direct the spiritual energies of increasing numbers of men and women.

In this atmosphere Robert Jaffray received his brief Bible school training. So far as we know there was nothing unusual about the young man's life during those days, no hint of the power that lay hidden within. He studied hard, worked to pay expenses and did some student preaching in Kenwood Heights, New York, at a little church that still likes to remember that it once had R.A. Jaffray as its pastor.

In 1897 A.B. Simpson got together another consignment of missionaries to send to the already opened South China field, and among them was Robert Jaffray. Another young man who went out with the group was Robert H. Glover, later to become famous as a world missionary. The two Roberts were sent together to Tung-un, a little town in Kwangsi, South China, where their first missionary work began.

The town did more for the missionaries than the missionaries did for the town. The work was not a success and was later abandoned, but while there the young men studied the difficult language and learned the ways of the Chinese firsthand. After a stay of only a year or so, they were sent to Wuchow, where their real missionary labors started in earnest.

In 1892 Rev. A.B. Simpson had visited China and had conducted a rather hasty survey of the field. The province of Kwangsi, in the great and thickly settled south of China, he found to be not only devoid of gospel light but bitterly opposed to the preaching of Christianity within its borders.

All foreigners were looked upon with suspicion. This general feeling against "foreign devils" had grown into open hostility, resulting in the murder of a French Roman Catholic priest. But the urgency of the need could not move him to throw his workers into mortal danger when such danger could be avoided. So he brought them into Canton, a relatively friendly city, and kept them there poised, waiting for the moment to enter Kwangsi. In 1897 the time seemed to be ripe. Open violence had died down, and though the Chinese were still unfriendly, no one wanted to wait longer. So a small band of missionaries entered the city of Wuchow.

They were allowed to enter, but that was as far as the Chinese would go. No one would rent them a house. Not a square inch of living space could they obtain, try as they would. For a time it looked as if the boycott was going to stop their plan head on, but then unexpectedly one of them turned up with the good news that he had found a place at last. They could move in at once. There was one slight drawback, hardly worth mentioning—the house was haunted. The superstitious Chinese would not go near the place. But the owner, who might or might not have believed in the reality of his invisible and nonpaying tenants, was willing to rent it to the foreigners. He could lose nothing by it, and if the white men and the ghosts could manage to hit it off together he might realize a bit of profit on the deal. So under these rather humorously dreadful conditions the Alliance missionaries settled in Wuchow and went to work.

To Wuchow, just two years after its opening, came Robert Jaffray. His headquarters continued to be located in Wuchow for the next 35 years. From there he carried on an ever-expanding program of missionary evangelism that ultimately took him as far south as Bali and as far east as New Guinea.

For the first few years Jaffray was just another Alliance missionary in Wuchow. In the annual report of the South China field he is mentioned only as a name on the roster. "R.A. Jaffray, 1897" the report said, and nothing more. Others were there ahead of him—Hess and Hinkey to mention two of them. Both of these were great men, strong-willed and aggressive, leaders in their own right. At first they somewhat overshadowed Jaffray.

Also on the field was Glover. Wherever he was, even in those early days, it was natural to accept him as the most prominent of the group. He did not seek a place or thrust himself forward, but because he was strong and gifted, others followed instinctively. His great natural ability and his grasp of world missions were such that after only a relatively short time on the field he was recalled to New York to become Foreign Secretary of The Christian and Missionary Alliance. He held this position with distinction for a number of years.

Robert Jaffray continued to labor on in South China, and with fuller maturity and wider experience came into greater and greater prominence. The hidden strength of the man and the smoldering zeal within him brought him naturally to the front. Over the years his influence increased, as did the confidence of his fellow missionaries in his inborn leadership. When it came time for the chairman, Rev. Isaac Hess, to retire, Jaffray was elected to the chairmanship of the South China field. This marked his real coming of age, and it was from then on that his notable work was accomplished.

5

Labors More Abundant

ONE OF THE FIRST PROJECTS to receive the loving attention of the new chairman was the Wuchow Bible School. This had been founded by Dr. Glover early in the development of the South China work, and now it became the object of Jaffray's zealous care. He was its principal for years. Under him it became a power for Christ in Kwangsi.

Jaffray believed with unquenchable faith in the importance of Bible schools in the total scheme of Christian missions. Wherever he went from those first days on, as soon as a few converts had been formed into a church, the next thing to receive his attention was the founding of a Bible school. For most of the years that he remained in Wuchow he taught in the school, usually lecturing to the entire student body. The material used in these lectures was later printed in the *Bible Magazine*, of which Jaffray was the editor, and was ultimately published in book form.

Believing in the power of the printed page, Jaffray kept the presses rolling, turning out tons of

Christian literature for distribution throughout the Orient. His publishing work was carried on with a zeal amounting to a crusader's passion. He had been reared in an atmosphere never free of the smell of printer's ink. The talk around the table had been of newspapers, the power of printed ideas and the influence of the press for good or evil, and he had not forgotten anything.

It was natural that he would—as soon as his new position as chairman made it possible—begin publishing in China. That was no easy job. There was no press available, no building to house it even if it could have been obtained, no pressmen to operate it and no provision in the budget to pay such a man even if one could be found.

Jaffray began as he usually did by trying to talk the home board into furnishing him with a press. When this failed, he appealed to interested friends in Canada and the United States. The response was so generous that before long he had a small publishing house named the South China Alliance Press going full blast. That was Jaffray's style—if the Society could not or would not provide something he felt he needed, he would beg for it from his friends and present it to the Society.

The Wuchow Bible School had been turning out students now for some years, sending them into active Christian work in various parts of China. Jaffray knew too well the incompleteness of their training and the urgent need for further education. They especially needed continuing contact with the school and with the missionaries. He had tried to meet the situation by writing letters and sending them out at regular intervals to the growing number of graduates. This suggested the idea of a publication that could have something of the personal touch of a letter along with a Bible teaching ministry. So the *Bible Magazine* was born.

It was Jaffray's *Bible Magazine* that first raised him to international prominence and made him known throughout the Far East. He maintained his own press, hired his own printers and clerical help and proceeded to turn out thousands of copies of the magazine for distribution throughout most of the countries in Asia. Of course the circulation was greatest in China itself, where the magazine was read by Christians of every denomination. But it also found its way into every part of the world where Chinese was read or spoken. It is interesting to learn that it even had some circulation in the United States, where it was read by respectable numbers of people, especially by the Chinese of San Francisco's Chinatown.

Jaffray was too well acquainted with the publishing business to allow his presses to turn out inferior pieces of work. The *Bible Magazine* was an excellent example of the printer's art, produced on good paper with fine layout and design. This was somewhat astonishing, considering the circumstances. Its contents were fully equal to the magazine's physical appearance. Written in Cantonese, its articles and editorial matters were altogether Biblical and evangelical. While there was a strong emphasis on prophecy, Jaffray was very sane in his interpretations and never indulged in rash forecasts nor sought to be wise above what was written. The influence of Jaffray's pen has been considerable, not only on the foreign field, but among Christians in many parts of the world. He did not content himself with one publication, but was forever writing, editing, printing matter of all kinds in many languages, always having to do with Christ and His message for the world. His literary style was colloquial. Fortunately he made no attempt at fine writing, but wrote to get something said, to persuade, to rouse someone to action. He was not writing for posterity, but to set power in motion for the all-important task of world evangelization. And this he accomplished with a remarkable degree of success.

Though Jaffray spoke Cantonese fluently, he was too wise to allow his Chinese writings to see the light before they had been corrected by someone to whom the language was native. He had a Chinese secretary who served for years as his literary right-hand man, smoothing out his awkward Cantonese and, when necessary, putting his Cantonese pieces into excellent English. In his publication work, as in everything else, Jaffray knew what he could do and what he could not do. He used the method of the modern giants of industry—he delegated labor. When he could not do a job, or did not have time, he knew where to find someone who could do it for him. He inspired it and directed it. That was his job. His helpers could supply the know-how and the skill. That was what he paid them for. The city of Wuchow was the headquarters of the South China field. Housed there, in addition to the publishing work and the Bible school, were a receiving home for missionaries and two orphanages, one for boys and another for girls. While each of these had its own director, Jaffray was the acknowledged head of all the work in Wuchow. His crusading zeal fired everyone around him. Out from Wuchow the missionaries went in every direction preaching the gospel in surrounding towns and villages.

The methods employed were simple and direct. Missionaries would go into a town and select a suitable spot, a market place or some corner where people gathered. They would try to back up against a wall to prevent attack from the rear. Then they would preach the Word for a while, and if they were able, would sing a few gospel songs. Whatever else might be done, though, they would always sell Scripture portions and hand out gospel literature to the crowds that gathered to hear them.

After the missionaries had been in town long enough to become established and to secure a hall for a meeting place, they would conclude by saying, "The meeting will continue in the hall. Come on in." Often the whole congregation simply moved inside the building and the service went right on. Usually the meeting was thrown open for questions—these people were not the "ignorant heathen" some people imagined, but rather they had behind them a culture older than the missionaries themselves had.

Over a long period of years Jaffray served as chairman of the South China field, pastor of the Wuchow church, principal of the Bible school, head of the South China Alliance Press, editor of the *Bible Magazine* and coordinator of the activities of the many workers on the field, both Chinese and foreign. Along with all this he managed to travel extensively, returning to Canada every three or four years for brief visits or making long journeys to act as interpreter for various English-speaking dignitaries who happened to be visiting China. And, of course, he was constantly exploring in one or another of the yet-unreached mission fields.

In the year 1900 Robert Jaffray married Miss Minnie Doner, an American missionary who had preceded him to South China by about two years. She was an excellent missionary. It was chiefly through her activities that the church was established in Wuchow. In addition to her regular missionary duties she also served for many years as matron of the receiving home. She shared her husband's labors faithfully, and as long as physically able, she aided immeasurably in accomplishing his multitudinous tasks.

6

The Man Jaffray

J AFFRAY WAS A GREAT MISSIONARY, but he was not
a foot soldier. Instead he was a missionary
general, a strategist and tactician of un-
doubted vision. But the actual labor of traveling
about and preaching in the villages had to be
done by others. He could do little itinerating. His
diabetes and his heart condition remained with
him—only his driving will enabled him to carry
on at all.

To meet the necessities of his weakened body,
he had to resort to means that might have appeared strange to anyone not familiar with the
circumstances. For instance, to conserve his
strength and outwit his tricky heart he rigged up a
desk that he could pull across his bed, hospital
fashion. This enabled him to do much of his
arduous work lying down. Commonly he would
be awake and at his labors by four o'clock in the
morning. When his breakfast was brought hours
later, he could be found surrounded by dictionar-
ies, commentaries and Bibles, with page after
page of finished manuscript piled beside him on
the bed.

For a person of his blazing energy, it was painful to be held down in that manner. A lesser man might have given up the fight. Everyone was waiting for him back in the homeland. Wealth, comfort, ease—all were his if he would agree to return to Canada and settle down. Had he done so, not a voice could have been raised against him, for he was a sick man. Common sense said that he did not belong in China. But he was a fighter, so he stayed on and got the work done. *How* he got it done was of little consequence.

For all his physical handicaps and his crushing burden for the world, Jaffray was never morbid nor hard to live with. Though of necessity he was often alone, he was by nature anything but a hermit. Whenever the circumstances would permit, he loved nothing better than to spend an evening with friends, letting himself out in story telling and boisterous humor.

One quality that made him especially beloved by his missionaries was his lowliness. Though in a position to be aloof, he was always a humble and approachable person. Rookie missionaries fresh from the homeland, green, awkward and ill at ease, would be received with as much enthusiasm as if they were among the world's great. The strangeness vanished instantly before Jaffray's friendly smile, and newcomers felt like they had always belonged to the family.

Once in private conversation with A.B. Simpson, R.R. Brown, then a young student, ventured to ask about the qualifications of a soul winner. "To be a great soul winner," Simpson replied, "a man must first be a great lover." It was only an impulsive sentence tossed off without too much thought, but it contains a world of spiritual philosophy. Spurgeon had a saying that a minister's congregation would always be the size of his heart. In at least one particular all spiritual leaders have been alike—they have all had large hearts. Nothing can take the place of affection. Those who have it in generous measure possess a magic power over men. Intellect will not do; Bible knowledge is not enough; even an upright life will be found wanting without this greatest of all gifts.

R.A. Jaffray was a great lover of people. His was not the detached love of the scientist or the student of ethnology. His love had in it almost no intellectual content. It was a vast sea of pure emotion that he never tried to analyze. He loved people for their own sakes and was drawn to them by an inward attraction bigger than reason. He was happy in the presence of human beings, whatever their race or color. He never had to "put up with" people—he enjoyed them too much to be bored with them. Indonesians, French, Dutch, white or yellow, high officials or coolies, he loved them all with artless affection. Those who came near to him felt that love like the warmth of the sun.

In Wuchow in 1907, a daughter, Margaret, was born to Robert and Minnie Jaffray. From the first moment his eyes fell upon her, she was the treasured darling of his heart. His love for her was a pure torrent that grew deeper and wider as the years passed. His letters in those days were filled

with ardent descriptions of his daughter's
charms. Some of these, written to the members of
his immediate family and never intended for publication, contain passages of almost lyric beauty.
To read these and gaze upon the family pictures
where Margaret always appears close to her
father's side is to feel an emotion bordering on
religious awe. Before this burning bush common
selfish people can only take off their shoes.

If we must analyze the man, if we must take his
soul apart to see what made him the great missionary he was, this would seem to be the answer
to our question. We hardly need explore further.
He loved God and all God's creatures. It was as if
there flowed within the heart of the man a rising
well of affection that *had* to find an object. Other
members of his family, relatives and friends—all
felt this. His letters abound with references to his
wife, all expressing his love for her. To his father
he wrote from every point of the compass letters
filled with deep, sincere affection. To his sister
Elizabeth, he wrote with a love almost boyish in
its simplicity.

As he grew older his passion to reach the lost
grew stronger, his vision widened and his purpose
narrowed. The walls of his office were hung with
huge maps over which he pored for hours like a
field marshall. Every issue of his magazines con-
tained maps, he lectured with maps before him
and he always talked of places and people who
waited for the light.

The huge amounts of work he was able to accomplish were possible only because he was a man who could exercise over himself a degree of discipline seldom seen in a person of his active nature. If asceticism is the rigid elimination of the superfluous in the interest of some higher purpose then Jaffray was an ascetic, but an ascetic without any of the morbidity usually associated with that term. If he "scorned delights and lived laborious days," it was not to gain merit in the sight of God or men, but to concentrate his powers for the mighty task before him.

Yet Jaffray had upon him none of the marks of the extremist. He was big, smiling and expansive, at ease in any company, ready with the friendly quip and to all appearances a man who very much enjoyed the world in which he lived. He was a man of two worlds, a brooding mystic whose eyes betrayed his deep absorption in things spiritual and heavenly, but he had succeeded in gearing his devotional life into the practical needs of this world and was never lost in fruitless contemplations.

If I might be permitted to create a term to describe Jaffray's spiritual type, I would call him an *extroverted mystic.* He had learned to pray as he moved. He conceived prayer and working as being identical acts. Work *was* prayer if it was God's work. I can think of only one man who accomplished this difficult fusion of the two acts—work and prayer—in the degree that Jaffray seems to have done: that was Brother Lawrence who taught "the practice of the presence of God."

With him, so he testified, the times of retirement were not greatly different from the times of work or travel. He had such a sense of the presence of God upon him that every common act was a prayer. This describes Jaffray precisely, and it accounts for his being able to be always in the Spirit *and* always on the go.

7

The Chair Presides

ONE OF THE GLORIES OF THE CHRISTIAN FAITH is its ability to adapt itself to every age and people without loss of essential power. Christ is the Son of Man and, as such, belongs not to the East or to the West but to the whole human race. He is every person's contemporary and is equally at home anytime and anywhere in the world.

The religion of Christ is like a light, pure in itself, but modified by the surface that reflects it. It was inevitable that the church in the Western world should have been influenced by our society's psychology. The sun shining upon a red or green surface will throw back a red or green light; so historically the church has taken certain peculiarities from the national and ethnic traits of those who have composed it. To be saved, the Lord does not require people to change their common ways—except so far as they may be contrary to simple righteousness—but permits them to live after the accepted customs of their own people.

It would have been well for the church if it had remembered this as it sought to carry truth across ethnic and cultural lines during the last hundreds of years. Too often it has confused pure Christianity with Christianity as modified by a particular culture. Its requirements for a person who desires to become a Christian have frequently followed a narrow and prejudiced conception of what constitutes a good life within one or another social bracket. Often missionaries have attempted unconsciously to make new converts good Canadians or Americans, forgetting entirely that the traits marking people as belonging to a particular nation have nothing whatsoever to do with Christ or salvation. Failure to take this into account has hindered the spread of the gospel in no small degree. The inability of the missionary to accept an alien culture as valid has created barriers to the Christian faith where no such barriers should ever have been erected.

To escape this difficulty and avoid the slowdown caused by cultural incompatibilities, the indigenous church has come into being. It is a philosophy of Christian missions that, stated briefly, means the church on the foreign field should be allowed to live and worship after its own manner without interference from outside. Along with this goes the idea of the autonomy of the national church—self-propagation, self-support and self-government.

Jaffray early came to the conclusion that he was sent to China not to make Westerners, but to make disciples. After that, their national customs should be respected and their rights to exist as a bona fide church should be taken for granted.

The Chinese church, he felt, should be just that—a Christian church in China, not a Western transplant within Chinese walls. This was his ideal, and to this he held throughout his long career.

Jaffray was a man of strong convictions when he knew his convictions were from the Lord. For all his apparent impetuosity, he moved slowly and prayerfully. With him prayer was not a religious duty, nor even a sweet enjoyment—it was his strength and guiding light. When he had not yet prayed a matter through he could be as cautious as any man, but when the day came that he felt he had found the mind of God he moved with bold assurance. On the question of the autonomy of the Chinese church he had no hesitation. Each church must be given full independence, and that at the earliest possible moment in its development. Of this he was certain.

Certain members of the South China conference stood against Jaffray on this. They held to the belief that each church should be made independent only when it had earned that right. A church that could not support itself, they felt, could not govern itself. Full autonomy, they argued with a good deal of logic, should come with full self-support. As long as a church accepted partial support from the mission board it should accept a certain amount of control from the board as well. Jaffray could never see this. He held out for full autonomy.

A compromise plan was finally worked out, which in theory gave the missionaries consider-

able authority over the Chinese churches that
were not yet self-supporting, but which in operation gave very little. These churches, it was decided, should be governed by three committees:
one to be composed altogether of Chinese Christians, another to be made up exclusively of foreign missionaries and the third to consist of an
equal number of missionaries and Chinese. According to this rather cumbersome arrangement
everyone would get a fair hearing and no par-
tiality would be shown in the administration of
affairs.

That was the way it appeared on paper, but one
factor had been overlooked—Jaffray's passionate
love for the Chinese. So mighty was the love that
it developed in him a marked pro-Chinese complex that he could never fully master. Let a differ-
ence arise between a missionary and a Chinese
person, and Jaffray would be, by a kind of instinct, on the side of the Chinese. Over the years
this led to some sharp differences between the
South China conference and its chairman.

It was inevitable that a man as strong-willed
and self-assured as R.A. Jaffray should sooner or
later run into trouble with his followers. Little
jealousies as well as honest differences of opinion
on matters of policy led occasionally to some
heated debates at yearly conferences. In present-
ing his plans to the conference, Jaffray's advantage lay in his acknowledged superiority plus the
fact that he was usually miles ahead of the rest in
his vision for the work. His weakness lay in his

intolerance of contrary views and his impatience with smallness wherever he found it.

Jaffray was a tremendously earnest man. His soul was possessed. The lost must hear the gospel—they *must* hear it. And the dark Pharaohs of the earth must hear the command, "Let my people go!" Alongside this burning imperative nothing else counted. It weighed on him like a debt, rode him like a conscience, became to him a holy obsession that would not let him rest day or night. In the grip of this mighty compulsion he was helpless, carried along by his overmastering passion for the souls of people.

To a man like Jaffray constitutional restrictions were an irritation, and when they blocked some plan to carry the gospel to the dying world they were an abomination, no less. He believed in the unity of the body and accepted constitutional government as best even for the mission field. But he was a prophet first, with a call and a commission. He had heard a Voice and had left all to follow it, and he found it hard to submit to the checks of lesser men. To get things done he was willing sometimes to set aside—or at least seriously strain—democratic process. This led occasionally to situations vexing as well as highly humorous.

On one occasion the members of the conference were debating whether they should or should not become responsible for the support and management of a certain children's home. Jaffray, as chairman, was supposed to be neutral where the Chinese children were concerned. When the time came to put the question forward, Jaffray demanded in a loud voice, "All in favor of throwing these poor helpless children out into the street say 'aye'." This manner of conducting business got things accomplished, but it did not make for good feeling among the missionaries.

That occasional rebellions developed among the workers cannot be denied, but Jaffray always came smiling through. He felt he knew the will of God and he would not be stopped by what he considered lack of vision on the part of his co-workers. It was a rugged way to do things, but it was excused in a measure by the fact that usually—though not always—subsequent events justified the chairman's wisdom.

His fellow-workers loved and trusted him, some of them with starry-eyed devotion. They were convinced of his sincerity and of his complete consecration to the will of God. He had nothing to gain by his labor but the joy of the finished task, and everyone who knew him knew that and loved him for it. Because of the oil on his forehead and the love in his heart they forgave everything else. The little disagreements soon healed over and were forgotten like summer showers, and the work went on and prospered.

8

In Peril of Robbers

ROBERT JAFFRAY MODESTLY SAID OF HIMSELF that he was never a man of courage, "but rather disposed to be timid and fearful." Events have a different story to tell.

The China of the 1920s was such as to demand courage or to force retirement. The province of Kwangsi was in a state of turmoil politically, confused and disordered to a degree challenging belief. Soldiers roved through the land, purportedly to defend the populace against robbers. But as happened constantly, they kidnapped, killed and robbed the very people they were supposed to protect.

Bands of armed robbers—sometimes running into the hundreds—scourged the country, burning and pillaging without mercy. If a soldier got tired of the army, or if his pay was slow in coming, he would as likely as not desert. Taking his uniform and guns with him, he would attach himself to some bandit chief and set out on a life of banditry without batting an eye. It was not uncommon to find at the head of a robber band a man who previously had been a high officer in the Chinese army.

In 1923 the city of Kweilin was subjected to a siege that lasted 77 days and brought the city to the point of starvation. Marshall Luh Long-Tin, an old robber chief now grown respectable, occupied the city when his sworn enemy, Gen. Shen Hung-Ying, rode up with a huge army and ordered him to come out and surrender. Of course the old gladiator refused, and the general promptly laid siege to the city. Fierce fighting raged back and forth for weeks and hundreds of people were killed. Parts of the city were burned to the ground; food became scarce and high in price. The poor in the city suffered intensely.

Within the besieged city were a number of foreigners, among them several Alliance missionaries: Walter Oldfield who had a marked genius for being there when troubled started but coming through in one piece and smiling, Rev. and Mrs. C.E. Lumpp and Rev. and Mrs. Joseph Cunningham. Through the long and terrible days of the siege they looked after the Chinese girls stranded in the Alliance school and gave help and encouragement as they were able.

One evening about two weeks after the start of the siege, some workmen came upon the body of Mr. Cunningham, lying quietly where it had fallen. He had been shot through the head by a stray bullet; whether by friend or foe no one ever knew. The sad little party laid their fallen comrade away with tears and prayers while the battle raged on and the fires roared around them.

Back at Wuchow Jaffray and his staff prayed for

the missionaries shut up in the beleaguered city. When the days increased to weeks, they decided to do something concrete to give body to their prayers. A little party was formed, consisting of Dr. Harry G. Mills and Rev. Edgar H. Carne of the Alliance, Rev. Rex Ray of the Southern Baptists and R.A. Jaffray. These men set out for Kweilin to try to effect a rescue, though just how this could be done was none too clear to any of them. They had traveled up the Fu River only a short distance when the little launch *Roanoke* that carried them was attacked by bandits. The soldiers—80 sent by the officials in Wuchow as an escort to march beside the boat on the shore—promptly melted away into the woods. The missionaries were left at the mercy of the robbers.

The Chinese outlaws were tough customers, like nothing any of the missionaries had ever seen before. "Some of them had eyes that glared like animals," Jaffray said later. "Their voices were rough and coarse like the growls of wild beasts." They snarled their demands for "toll," a euphemism for plunder. They carried knives and guns, and they meant business.

Jaffray as usual took over. He demanded to talk to their chief. "We are missionaries," he told the chieftain. "You have no right to ask a toll of us. We *receive* offerings to help us with our work. Come now, be reasonable. Give us an offering and let us go." The sheer brass of the man had its effect, as he knew it would. From that time on the robbers treated him with respect. He had spoken

the only language these men of blood and violence could understand—the language of courage.
But they had no intention of letting him go.

After stripping the launch of everything that
was not nailed down and taking from the missionaries all but the clothes they had on, the robbers
put them under guard and started with them into
the mountains. It was kidnapping, and the object
was ransom.

Brute courage will take a person a long way, but
there comes a time when it is not enough, when a
person of mere physical daring meets his or her
match in one of deeper moral courage. These robbers glorified rude force and lived by violence, yet
they had not been long in the presence of Robert
Jaffray before they knew they had met a man who
was their superior. Jaffray spoke of this later as if a
bit astonished at his own boldness. He attributed
the whole thing to God, and talked about it, without a trace of pride, as if it had concerned someone else.

"I have never seen such wicked men in my life,"
he said, "and never want to see such again. I
could never have believed that men and women—
for there were women there, too—could sink to
such utter depths of depravity. But I found that I
could look these fierce, wicked men straight in
the face, put my hands on their shoulders and
talk to them about the Lord Jesus without a
tremor in my voice and without the slightest consciousness or appearance of fear. This seemed to

be as much of a surprise to them as it was to me, and it appeared to trouble them."

The moral ascendancy of Jaffray secured for the missionaries a deep respect and made the cruel, gruelling climb into the mountains considerably easier for all of them than it might otherwise have been. At best it was hard going, with little to eat and with aching muscles and tired, blistered feet. Jaffray himself, however, declared that he came through the ordeal with his shoes intact and with never a blister on either foot. As usual he gave the glory to God, and in order that credit might go where credit was due, he also mentioned gratefully the brand of shoes he was wearing. That was always Jaffray's way. They were good shoes, one gathers from his remarks, but God had seen to it that he had on that kind of shoes when the emergency arose.

And all the while they were struggling on, fording rivers, climbing slippery banks, diving into ditches when the robbers feared someone was approaching, crawling upward on hands and knees. Even after they had arrived at the filthy, smoke-blackened cave of the outlaws, Jaffray was in moral command of the wretched crew. As he chose he intimidated them, made them ashamed, had them doubled up with laughter at his daring wit or had them wiping away tears from their hardened faces as he preached to them of Jesus and His love. "I talked to them," he said, "until their hearts were moved and tears came to their eyes. I found that the love of Jesus and His vicarious death on the cross was the theme that seemed to touch the tender spot in their hearts."

Between spells of revelling, gorging themselves with stolen food and performing unashamed public acts of bestial lust, they conferred about the prisoners and the ransom. They finally decided to release Jaffray and Miller, sending them back to Wuchow with a demand for a ransom of $300,000 while they held the other hostages. Jaffray argued with them, rebuked them, preached to them and promised them nothing except that he would present their demands in Wuchow. Then he left. "Don't forget that Christ loves you," he said as he was leaving. "Don't forget the ransom money," they shouted in reply as he disappeared down the trail.

The money was finally raised by the Chinese officials, and the intrepid Mr. Oldfield was chosen to deliver the ransom and convey the prisoners back to the city. Out he rode, attended like a king by an escort of *robbers*. When he arrived at the outlaw's camp he found that Mr. Ray had slipped through the fingers of the guards some days before and was gone. Carne was still there, sick, emaciated and too weak to walk. Oldfield managed to bring him back to Wuchow, where he soon recovered.

A singular—and to the person of faith, significant—circumstance must be mentioned in connection with this adventure. The physical strain through which the members of the party passed was so severe that the toughened robbers themselves were often near exhaustion as they fought on day by day up the gnarled sides of the mountains and over the cruel terrain. Jaffray had nursed an ailing heart from his childhood, and as he admitted, when the trek began the first thing he thought about was whether or not his heart would take the ordeal. Yet when the whole thing was over and he was back again at his desk he found that he had actually benefited from the experience. His condition was definitely improved, and while he never became entirely well, he enjoyed better health from that time forward.

9

Toward the South

EVERY NOTABLE ADVANCE IN THE SAVING WORK of God among men will, if examined, be found to have two factors present: several converging lines of providential circumstances and a person.

When God brought Israel out of Egypt He first set the stage by a combination of circumstances and then called forth His man. For a long time— indeed, a lifetime—He had been readying him, and Moses was prepared to step forward instantly when his moment arrived. Every student of church history knows how many lines converged on Martin Luther. Without the work of the re- formers who preceded him he could never have accomplished his world-shaking task. But it is equally true that without him the work of those others might have been largely wasted.

This takes no proper honor from anyone. Who can tell how often in the past God prepared the setting for some gracious work of love and could find no one to act for Him in the hour of need? "I looked for a man," said the Lord upon one un- happy occasion, "but I found none." And who can tell how many "mute inglorious Miltons" there may have been, fully able to perform largely upon the stage of history, but who were born out of due time—great workers without a ready work? It is a blessed thing when a person is found to do a work of God, to catch the scattered parts prepared by others and weld them into a perfect whole.

The spiritual importance of the work of R.A. Jaffray in French Indochina is so vast that its development deserves a separate study if we want to learn the ways of God in His quest for souls. The inevitable factors are there—the long preparation, the work done by others and then the person chosen to carry the task through to completion.

In the book *After Fifty Years*, Robert Ekvall writing of the opening of the French Indochina field says:

> But in those years from 1887 to 1911 God in His inscrutable providence was making a great and mighty preparation for a period of service which was to be so speeded up with both extensive activity and intensive accomplishment, that 25 years was to witness a growth which a century of effort had not seen on some fields. One aspect of the preparation was the extension of French power, culture and language over the area, the creation of a stable, reputable government with its assurance of law and order. Roads were opened up through the land to transport rubber and coffee and for military purposes. These were to

become highways to speed the gospel. Savage
warring tribes were brought under the same
sort of law that made a hearing for the gospel
when the first missionaries of the cross followed the Roman legions to land on British
soil.

There it is: the pattern repeated so often in history—a preparation made all without knowledge
or intention by the great of the earth, revealed
afterwards to have been the sovereign working of
God in His purposes for the world. As the missionaries went in with the gospel, "French power
made a way, and French justice reached into the
jungle to protect them." And toward this provi-
dence another line was reaching: God was groom-
ing someone to take advantage of the circumstances—many people, in fact, for Jaffray was not
alone in his vision for French Indochina. He was
heir of a burden carried for years by noble-
hearted men and women who had been toiling
in South China, just across the border from the
promised land.

Though Jaffray was the instrument whom God
honored above all others in the work of missions
in Indochina, he never took credit for the work
nor for the original vision. As early as 1887 Simpson had begun to look toward Indochina, then
called Annam. In 1892 David LeLacheur, an Alliance missionary, had visited Saigon. Seeing
Simpson in Singapore a year later, he fired him
further with the desire to enter that neglected

field. Jaffray himself, only a year after coming to South China, had become restless and had taken a jaunt into Tonkin, down the Red River as far as Hanoi, hoping to get at least a small foothold there. Nothing came of this, but Jaffray had spied out the land. It was more than a map to him now.

A year later, meeting Mr. and Mrs. Sylvan Dayan in the United States, he persuaded them to cross the ocean and enter Tonkin at once. They were French Canadians, and as Jaffray saw it, they would for that reason have favor with the French officials. He was playing his wisdom against the prejudices of the officials. At the turn of the century the Dayans crossed over into Tonkin and set to work. Again nothing permanent resulted. Jaffray was God's man, but for the time being he was running ahead of the cloudy pillar.

Later the South China conference established a station at Lung Chow, on the Tonkin border, with the intention of jumping from there over into the land. But this was forbidden by the officials. And so it went for years. Always they were trying, and always they were being turned back, as if Christ was saying, "My time is not yet come." So they could only wait, and waiting was always hard for Jaffray.

But the internal pressure was becoming too great. Something had to give way soon. Jaffray, we have said, was not alone in his vision. All the missionaries in South China were ready to help, to go if necessary, but also to give their backing whether they went or stayed.

At last the Cloud seemed to be lifting. Lloyd
Hughes and Paul Hostler were selected to go over
into the land and see what could be done. Jaffray
went along to act as contact person. This was
decided by common consent—Jaffray was the
person and no one in South China could have
fulfilled his precise task. He was the perfect diplo-
mat. He was suave, dressed well and carried himself like a prince. He knew no stranger and feared
no man's face. So the three men entered Tourane
and set up their banner. This time the gospel was
here to stay, they hoped. And so it was, as subsequent events confirmed.

Hughes never lived to see the work get more
than a small start. Shortly after this he made a
trip back to China and suddenly died there. Hostler settled down in Tourane and set to work to
learn the language. Jaffray resumed his duties in
Wuchow, but his heart was glad. The Alliance
was now operating in Indochina.

A thriving church was soon established in
Tourane, followed immediately by an outstation
in Faifoo. Missionaries were coming down from
South China, and others were coming from the
homeland to add to their number. Simpson's
dream was coming true before Jaffray's eyes.
Town after town was visited with the message of
life, and many were hearing the gospel for the first
time. The day was breaking in Indochina.

10

Stopped by War

SUDDENLY ON THE OTHER SIDE OF THE WORLD a global war broke loose. The French were in the center of the storm. Soon the Kaiser's hordes had trampled Belgium under their feet and were driving toward Paris with every likelihood of taking it. French Indochina was agog. The loyal French there were straining to be as good citizens as the ones at home. They tried to help the cause by suspecting everyone. Mistrust and hate filled the air.

Harmless old Isaac Hess, who had lived in the heavenlies so long he had all but forgotten his earthly nationality, was suspected of being a German sympathizer. Hostler's name, too, sounded suspicious. In a frenzy of nationalism the French officials padlocked the mission stations and forbade the preaching of the gospel in Indochina. Two missionaries, whose names grated unpleasantly upon loyal French ears, were banished from the field. Two others went with them. The rest could stay—but they must not preach the gospel or attempt to spread their doctrines. The work in French Indochina had suddenly ceased.

But the French officials had not reckoned with

the Host. The church in Annam would not go down defeated. When it could not operate openly, it went underground. Native workers took over. The missionaries could do no more than sit tight, study the language and wait for the war to end. But the Annamese Christians went right on with the work. Conversions occurred constantly and the work grew with incredible rapidity. As time passed and the turbulent emotions of the people leveled out somewhat, the officials began to note the wholesome moral effect of Christianity upon the people. They were pleased in spite of themselves and gradually came to look with approval upon the work of the Alliance.

In 1916 Jaffray was elected superintendent of the French Indochina field. His headquarters were to remain in Wuchow, but now he would be in a position to spark the new field to success. One of his first moves was to visit the French Governor-General in Indochina. The war was still on and the name of the French General Joffre was on everyone's lips. Jaffray neatly turned this to account. To the Governor-General he suggested casually that the names *Joffre* and *Jaffray* were so much alike that they just might be distantly related.

The governor smiled, but he was interested. He wanted to say yes to this affable foreigner, but he was only free within certain limits. He would be responsible for whatever occurred. After some hesitation he consented to lift the ban and permit the preaching of the gospel in Indochina. To be safe he refused to put anything in writing. Permission was verbal only. The official had only one good eye, the left one being blind. "You go ahead," he told the missionary, "and I won't see you. When a missionary appears I'll put my hand over one eye—the right one."

Jaffray left the governor's office walking on air. But his troubles were not over. Difficulties began to develop almost at once. The missionaries were to learn that officials change, and their minds change, too, with any chance shift in the political winds. Situations soon developed in the work that seem from this distance to have been wholly without reason or common sense. Decisions made against the missionaries were so arbitrary and whimsical as to create the impression that some playful devil with a flair for practical jokes had been commissioned to wear out the servants of God and to bring the work to a stop from sheer exhaustion.

The quality of Jaffray's generalship was tested during that bizarre period in the mission's history, and the patience of his workers was tried to the breaking point. They could go here, but they could not go there. This city was a French colony, that one a possession, and the other one a protectorate. Now they could preach here but not there, and soon it would be all right to preach there but not here. And all this was so wholly arbitrary and out of order that Jaffray, who loved order and admired forthrightness, was pressed out of measure. Against the caprice of the unpredictable French

officials he had no refuge but God. And to God
he took his case patiently and insistently until he
won it.

Prayer and patience at last conquered where
armies might have failed. One after another of
the provinces and cities were freed of hindrances
until French Indochina came to be very much an
occupied country, with Jaffray and his missionaries as the benign conquerors.

Indochina was not a single country, but a group
of states or provinces, differing from each other in
race, language and culture. Each had to be handled in its own way. For instance, to preach the
gospel to the various peoples, the missionaries
had to know as many as 11 languages. This meant
endless work to translate the Scriptures, to print
them and to make them accessible to the people.

Almost as soon as official permission had been
obtained to operate in Indochina, the first printing press was set in motion there. It was established in Hanoi, the capital, and was named Mission Press. As the work grew, hymnals, tracts,
books, devotional and doctrinal literature of all
kinds came rolling from the Mission Press—the
superintendent of the field was still Robert Jaffray,
the son of the publisher of the Toronto *Globe*. His
faith in the printed page never diminished but
grew as his experience widened.

Qualified members of the Alliance staff worked
steadily on translating the whole Bible into Annamese. This was something of a monumental
work in its own right and took the better part of 10

years to complete. When it was at last printed and given to the people, it came as a burst of light in the darkness. Its appearance helped to stabilize the fluid Annamese tongue, giving to it a permanence of form in a small way comparable to that given to the English language by the King James Bible.

11

The Jaffray Pattern

RIGHT HERE SEEMS AS GOOD A PLACE AS ANY to look at the Jaffray philosophy of Christian missions. It was a simple philosophy based on New Testament principles and shot through with salty common sense. From it he evolved a pattern for his work, a pattern that shows through everything he did from his earliest South China days to the end of his life.

It is doubtful that Jaffray ever sat down and reasoned out a policy. His mind did not work that way. He scooped his ideas on the move as a swallow at evening takes its supper on the wing. The Bible and a sound instinct guided him, and hard experience corrected any flaws in his theories. His views were never complex nor difficult to comprehend. The work of missions was fairly simple after all. It consisted chiefly of four things to do: contact, evangelize, organize and instruct. That was all. But in the doing of these essentials a person might toil a lifetime. Nevertheless his or her toil would be fruitful because these were things Christ had sent His servants to do.

Contact was first. Nothing could be done until communication had been established. The missionary must go to the lost tribes. This was the basal tenet in Jaffray's missionary creed, and to him it was the voice of command. It created within his mind an eager restlessness that never left him. The sight of a map or the sound of a foreign name stirred him as the sound of an alarm bell stirred the old fire horse of yesteryear. Jaffray was a pioneer, an explorer, an adventurer obsessed with the urge to discover new peoples and hidden tribes.

It is this aspect of missionary work that captures the imagination of the public. We are all children enough to love the thrill of missionary adventure enjoyed by proxy, and Jaffray knew this. As a good showman he was willing to give the people at home what they wanted to hear. His newsletters and magazine articles often read like real tales of the wild, but they were never told for their own sake nor for mere amusement. Jaffray was altogether too serious for any such child's play. If he could win attention with honest reports of exotic customs and curious ways of strange people, he was not adverse to doing it, but his motives were always in full view. He wanted help. He wanted money—lots of it—but more than anything he wanted young people to hurry over and help him with the job. And they came, these young people, winged with prayer and backed with the consecrated wealth of the people at home.

After contact came evangelization. Christ had told His disciples to go into all the world and

make disciples. To Jaffray that could only mean
one thing—win lost people to Christ now, bringing them to trust Him as their personal Savior at
once, without waiting for Western influences or
long courses of instruction to condition them.
They had but to hear the gospel and they could
be saved, if they wanted to be, as certainly as any
Westerners could.

That was Jaffray's theory, and its soundness
was confirmed in person-to-person practice. It
worked—that was the glory of it. Lives were actually changed overnight, transformed by this simple technique. People could and did jump into the
kingdom of God in one bound, and for the most
part those who made the great transition lived to
prove that the change was real and permanent.

The next step was to organize these new Christians into a church. It would need to be simple at
first, little more than a loose, common-consent
organization with certain people among them
picked to act as leaders, giving direction to the
group. Later it could go on to a more perfect form
of organization with a pastor, deacons and elders.
But that could wait, for the missionary would act
as the real leader until the new converts had been
instructed. Ecclesiastically minded people may
smile at this, but it worked—and it still works—
and that fact cannot be smiled away.

The new church, then, must be taught the great
truths of the Christian faith. It must be instructed
and indoctrinated. To accomplish this, two
means were required: the school and the printing

press. These came after organization and, where Jaffray could have his way, not long after.

The printing press was to Jaffray what handwritten epistles were to Paul—a means of keeping in touch with his converts as they increased in number and as distances made personal contact impossible. The press also made available to these new Christians the best in spiritual literature. Jaffray's presses usually turned out matter written by himself and addressed to particular needs. But they also produced books, tracts, magazines, Bible courses and expositions of one after another of the books of the Bible as he could prepare them and as he felt the people were ready to receive them.

Along with the printing press stood the Bible school as an effective instrument for the dissemination of the truth. Jaffray believed in the Bible school with a positiveness amounting to sheer dogmatism. He knew its power and promoted it with unremitting zeal. Foreign missionaries would never be the last word in the evangelization of any country. The best and swiftest work would always be done by Christian nationals operating among their own people. But these must first be taught, established in the truth and trained for the most effective service. The Bible school could do this—no other agent could. So every field must have a school—at least one, and more if the need demanded. That was Jaffray's view, and again its soundness was confirmed in practical outwork.

The speed with which the Christian faith

spread among previously unreached people testifies to the fact that Jaffray's vision was divinely given. He would never allow his workers to huddle together. They were expected to spread out and stay on the move. He was so insistent upon this that some of his workers at times questioned his wisdom, and a few dared to oppose him outright. Usually subsequent developments justified him, however, and the doubters were forced to acknowledge that he had been right.

"Of course," said one official before whom he appeared to request permission to preach the gospel, "you will concentrate your forces?"

"Certainly," Jaffray agreed quickly. Then stepping to the wall where a huge map of the country hung, he touched with his finger one after another spot on the map. "We'll concentrate here, and here, and here, and here."

"Why, how many missionaries have you?" asked the astonished official.

"Six," replied Jaffray, unsmiling.

It was this strategy of "concentrating" all over the map that gave such thrust to his missionary service.

In spite of the blitz-like speed of advance, he never fell into the error of believing he had done the Lord's work merely by announcing the gospel and moving on. He would not leave the new Christians to fall back into their old ways. Wherever a few converts were made a church must be formed; gains must be consolidated. Then the messenger could go on, and not until then. This

was wisdom and it was New Testament proce-
dure. It might well serve as a pattern for all missionary societies everywhere.

The notion that we have only to announce the
gospel once to each tribe and then pass on to the
next without regard to results is as old as it is
false. Though it is the philosophy behind much
present-day missionary enterprise, it is nevertheless a plain heresy of method based upon a mis-
reading of orders. It is interesting to know that
Wesley and his Methodists had to face this in
their early missionary activities, and it is instruc-
tive to learn how they handled it.

One section of the old Methodist Discipline,
published in 1848 bears—I would guess—the
marks of Wesley's own thinking, which preceeded
it. Under the head "Rules by which we should
Continue, or Desist from, Preaching at any
Place," the question is asked, "Is it advisable for
us to preach in as many places as we can without
forming any societies?" The answer is emphatic.
"By no means. We have made the trial in various
places; and that for considerable time. But all the
seed has fallen by the wayside. There is scarcely
any fruit remaining."

Jaffray was of Presbyterian stock, and it is
doubtful whether he ever gave much attention to
the ways of the early Methodists. But in the hot
fires of experience he learned the same lessons
they had learned before him and he arrived at the
same conclusions. This may not be the last word
that can be spoken on the subject, but wise

missionaries listen respectfully to these masters. They bring to the support of their philosophy the unanswerable argument of overwhelming success.

12

The Conquest of Indochina

FOR ANY WHO MIGHT BE TEMPTED TO DOUBT that the Lord works today as He did in the time of the Apostles, a little familiarity with the history of Alliance work in Indochina should be good medicine. The wonders of the work can never be fully told, but the sketchiest outline is enough to suggest comparison with the book of Acts.

From the beginning the work showed signs of more than human effort. Obviously Jaffray had followed the Cloud and had gone in under the blessing of God. Not logic but a compelling urge had led the way into Indochina. Plain cold facts, indeed, were against the move, for to get to Tonkin and Annam he had to bypass millions of Chinese and tribes who had not yet been evangelized. But how can reason be compared to the leading of the Holy Spirit? Jaffray felt he had such guidance, and no doubts ever troubled him.

Jaffray never resided for any length of time in Indochina. His headquarters were in Wuchow and from there he directed affairs in the new field, making periodic visits as needed. His work in South China was a full-time job for the average person and the weight of the new field added tremendously to his load. There can be no denying that the whole thing spread him out considerably further than his strength would allow. Some concern began to be felt by the missionaries of South China, but the conference was not willing to let him step down. Year after year he continued to be elected chairman of the field. The spiritual size of the man made this inevitable, for he was always a man of prayer, vision, foresight and courage. Everyone felt that his equal was not among them.

In order that the conference might continue to enjoy the admitted advantage of such leadership as Jaffray offered and still not allow the details of the work to suffer, a vice chairman was chosen. This person was to be invested with the responsibilities as the chairman would ordinarily carry, but which Jaffray, under the circumstances, was unable to fulfill. The conference choice was Walter Oldfield, an experienced man who was remarkably active, who could thrive on tough assignments and to whom hardships, perils and long, arduous journeys were simply nothing at all. The arrangement was a happy one. Any deficiency in the actual work of the chairman was more than supplied by the energetic vice chairman, and Jaffray was set free to pray, to dream, to consult maps and to plan his conquests into new territory. And Oldfield was serving his apprenticeship for when he would be called to fill the office of chairman of the South China field.

The Alliance work in Indochina enjoyed an unusually fine staff of missionaries. This might have been expected—every superior person has the ability to call around him or her other superior people. There is a magnetism about a strong person that attracts others of the kind. Many of those who labored under Jaffray's command were great workers in their own right—spiritual, wise, gifted and wholly abandoned to God and the cause of missions. They accepted sacrifice as a necessary part of the job and thought little of it. This undoubtedly had much to do with the high level of moral and spiritual power that marked and still marks the church in Indochina.

The story of the progress of the gospel in Indochina is wonder-filled. For swiftness, intensity and scope it has few equals since the days of the apostolic church. Special providences, miracles, precise timings, sufferings, courage, grace and blazing zeal were all there in abundant measure.

In his book *With Christ in Indo-China*, Rev. E.F. Irwin says,

> Those early Christians had great faith in God. They expected interpositions of divine power on their behalf, and they received them. Miracles similar to those recorded in the Book of Acts were enacted before their eyes, not because of the faith of the missionaries, but because of the faith of these 'babes in Christ'

who expected from their newly found Savior greater power than they had thought belonged to their old enemy the devil.

These Christians were acutely God-conscious. They habitually walked close to the borders of another world. While our timid doubts may cause us to draw back slightly at some of the things that occurred among them, simple honesty compels us to admit that their spirit was nearer to that of the Bible than our own staid and proper godliness will ever be. A wall of prayer had broken over them, as if a dam somewhere upstream had suddenly given way, and the resultant flood was too great for ordinary channels to contain. It overflowed the banks and produced unusual happenings.

A man of the city of Cantho, Cochin China, before he had heard as much as one word of the Christian message, had a vision or dream in which he saw a strange man—a foreigner—preaching a new religion. Irwin writes:

In his dream he became convinced that this was the true way of life, and that the God of whom this foreigner preached was the One whom he should worship. He forsook his idolatry and followed only the idea that he had gotten from this vision, until one day in Cantho he met the missionary who had recently opened a station there. He gladly listened to the gospel message and became one of the first Christians in Cantho.

How shall we interpret this? That will depend upon our spiritual viewpoint, but I am quite sure that if this story were done in King James English and inserted in Acts the casual reader would detect in it no variance from the ordinary mood of that book.

Let me repeat in attempted Elizabethan—the language of the King James Bible—a story written in Irwin's history of Alliance missions in Indochina:

> And it came to pass that as they journeyed a young man met them having an unclean spirit: and he threw himself on the ground, gnashing his teeth and foaming. And they essayed to talk with him, but they could not, for he was dumb. And it was so that the multitudes ran. Together the disciples commanded the unclean spirit and said: "Thou deaf and dumb spirit, we charge thee, come out of him." And straightway the spirit leaveth him and he fell to the ground and became as one dead. And as the people wondered he arose and stood upon his feet and went unto his own house, and they marvelled greatly. And so much the more they published it abroad what had been done unto him that had an unclean spirit.

Would this story seem out of place if found in

one of the Gospels? I think not. Yet only the language has been borrowed from the New Testament—the facts themselves actually occurred under the eyes of Alliance missionaries in Siam. Such happenings as these, if they were not common, were certainly not uncommon in Indochina. The work was carried on with fiery enthusiasm. Many of the workers from that field when back home for short furloughs manifested a spirit of revival unusual even among Alliance missionaries. They had seen the Lord's wonders among the unreached, and their whole demeanor gave evidence of it.

As for "interpositions of divine power," wonders and miracles of deliverance, Jaffray accepted them as a matter of course, something to be expected where men and women were moving forward under the direction of the Holy Spirit. He was in the right sense a sophisticated man of the world, but his faith was as simple as a child's. He met every challenge with prayer, and when he had taken some knotty problem before the Lord, he counted upon an answer. That answer would be figured into his total plan for the work, and the success of his plans over the years suggests that answers to prayers were surprisingly frequent. They had to be. The work could never have been done without them.

But the work was done, an amazing work considering the difficulties. For there were always difficulties, and many of them were so serious as to discourage any hope of success—an unfriendly climate, little money, official prohibitions, a chronic shortage of workers, huge distances and poor transportation. Laos, for instance, was the largest of the states in Indochina, but its inhabitants numbered less than one million, and these were a conglomeration of people of many different languages and ethnic backgrounds scattered throughout a land-locked and mountainous country. In Cambodia, Buddhism dominated and all who turned to Christ there at once became objects of fierce and fiery persecution.

These were but a few of the hindrances. Each corner of the field had its own peculiar obstacles, yet so mighty was the spiritual impulse at work that nothing could stop the triumphant march of truth. Everywhere the work prospered. Converts were baptized by the hundreds, churches were established and city after city opened to the gospel.

Jaffray watched over these churches as Paul watched over his converts in Galatia or Thessalonica. And he always kept before him the idea that they must spread out, that they must move on, over the next river, across the next mountain to contact more and more souls for Christ.

13

The Hong Kong Incident

A S JAFFRAY GREW OLDER HIS WORK TOOK ON more and more the character of a military campaign. He himself was in top command, and he never let his workers forget it. They were his "soldiers"—for them he would fight to the finish, but they must give him three things: obedience, cooperation and hard work. Upon these he insisted with the severity of a military commander.

As for hard work, it was never difficult to secure this, for the missionaries had constantly before them in the person of their leader a living example of ceaseless activity and self-sacrificing toil. He demanded much, but he never asked more than he himself gave.

Cooperation was something else again, for the workers were strong-willed men and women with minds of their own, and some of them did not take too kindly to close supervision. Besides, it must be admitted that Jaffray was not a shining example of perfect cooperation.

This was especially true of his relationship with

74

the home board. He always went through the motion of consulting the board, it is true, but he did not always wait for their answer. He was on the field, he argued, in intimate touch with things, while the board was back in the States. What could they know about his problems? Besides, it sometimes took as long as three months to get a ruling from the board—they only met four times a year—and the needs on the field were often so acute they could not wait three days.

Such delays, he felt, were intolerable. The hard-pressed members of the board back in New York did the best they knew how, circumstances being what they were. They wanted to work with Jaffray, but they had 19 other fields to look after, and he was prone to forget this.

When it came to obedience the rule was iron-clad. Jaffray would tolerate no rebellion among his missionaries. When a person had been assigned to a field and given a job, for instance, he or she must stay on the field and do that job. There would be no appeal and there must be no refusal. For the most part this worked out perfectly, but there could be exceptions.

There was a time in China when some of the workers dared to ignore the authority of the field chairman. It was 1925 and China was in a state of near-revolution. The lives of missionaries were in peril and a number of them were sent to Hong Kong and told to lie low under British protection until the heat was off.

Certain of the big steamship companies had

ships lying in Hong Kong ready to sail but unable
to move from their docks for want of crews for
them. Through the newspapers the owners hast-
ily issued a call for help. To any able-bodied man
they offered a three-month trip to the United
States or Canada, with time out for a short visit
after making port, and passage back guaranteed.
All they asked in return was a little work on board
ship—no experience necessary.

The missionaries had been compelled for weeks
to remain inactive, and there was no sign of a
break for a long time to come. So some of them
decided to take a trip home. No harm could come
of it and anything was better than sitting still.
Eight missionaries signed on and sailed out of
Hong Kong.

In a few weeks they returned as they had
planned, but no open arms welcomed them back
to China. Jaffray had placed every one of them on
the blacklist and would have absolutely nothing
more to do with them. Two of them, by properly
humbling themselves, did manage after a while to
get themselves reinstated. The rest were never admitted again to the conference, and either drifted
back to the States or joined other societies in
China. Men capable of that kind of conduct,
Jaffray reasoned, were unfit for missionary work.
One could never tell what they might do in an
emergency.

Jaffray has been censored for this rather high-
handed act. But whoever would condemn him is
compelled at the same time to place upon an

apostle the mark of disapproval—Paul did exactly the same thing in a similar circumstance. He blacklisted Mark for going back from the work and refused to travel with him anymore.

Such methods as we have described never look good on paper. When examined merely as theories they are vulnerable to attack from every direction, but the big test is, after all, success. And Jaffray, in the words of one who had worked with him, "was a wizard at getting things done." Add to this almost incredible ability to accomplish his ends, a warm, loving personality and a general air of mystic detachment and we have the explanation of his hold upon the confidence and affections of his fellow workers. They might shake their heads at times, but they sensed upon this big, smiling, hard-working man the unmistakable oil of anointing. They would follow the man with the oil, even if they did not agree with his methods; and the fruit that attended their labors was sufficient proof that they were not far wrong in their choice.

Thinking upon it from this distance, the work Jaffray did was large, and we of lesser accomplishments might feel deeply gratified to have to our credit half as much. But to him it was never enough. His vision so far outran his deeds as to keep him forever dissatisfied. The few workers allowed him from year to year, the modest budget, the relatively small number of conversions as seen against the staggering numbers yet unconverted—these things weighed on him and brought from him some of the most plaintive and eloquent utterances to be found anywhere in the literature of Christian missions.

By 1925, for instance, the Alliance had 77 stations already in operation in Kwangsi. From these the gospel was radiating in every direction. That appears well on the pages of a yearly report, but it never suggested to Jaffray the idea of self-congratulation. Within that province were 83 cities and 1,533 market towns. All self-satisfaction disappeared before the chairman's tragic question, "What are 77 stations among these?"

Jaffray never underestimated the value of what was being done on his field. He told it far and wide to whoever would listen, but he was careful to tell it in such a way as to lead to greater activity rather than to complacency. However wonderful it might appear to the people back home, to him it was but a good beginning, a proof of what might be done and a challenge to stepped-up endeavor.

Jaffray, as we have indicated before, lived from a spring within him deeper than mere intellect. The logic of foreign missions was never out of his mind, and he could use it with telling force when addressing an audience. But it took more than bare logic to drive this man as he was driven for about 50 years of his life. Reasons he could always give, reasons so hard and hot that they were like an artillery barrage, but no one would quite be convinced that these accounted for his work as a Christian missionary. There was something else present, something bigger and finer than reason, something that compelled him to go to the lost regardless of what was logical.

It was this mystic something that, when the last word is said, accounted for the missionary Jaffray. The man owed much to heredity—his fine bearing, his easy suavity, his startling good looks and his driving personality were all part of the legacy left him by his ancestors. The staunch moral strain with him may have owed something to his Scottish blood. But the noble obsession that made him a missionary pioneer never came from Adam's flesh—it took rise in the heart of God.

When seen in this perspective, the Hong Kong incident is easily understood. It accords with the total of Jaffray's life. The work of God, as he saw it, was bigger than men. A little had been done, a few lost sheep had been gathered in, but all China teemed with millions more who yet stood in the deep shadows of sin and death. These must be reached at any cost to himself or any other Christian soul. To leave the work even for a day was shocking to his heart. He would never do it himself, nor would he forgive it in his fellow missionaries.

14

The Cloud Is Taken Up

THE LAST YEARS OF JAFFRAY'S STAY in South China were troubled ones. Politically, all of China was in an uproar. Looking back on it we are hard put to discover exactly what was taking place during those times. It was civil war, but not the sort with which we are familiar in history where one side is drawn up against another in some kind of understandable order. Instead everyone appeared to be against everyone else, and it was never very clear just why. The entire country seemed to be tearing apart at the seams. Of this, Jaffray wrote:

> Poor China is in a condition of confusion and chaos. Throughout the whole country contending military factions are in mortal combat. There seems to be no real principle at stake in any of these wars. One leader is about as good as another. All are moved by personal selfish motives. Satan is behind the scene and fills the atmosphere with the spirit of conflict and bloodshed. He puts into peo-

ple's hearts positive delight in war, plunder and murder.

China had not been long in this condition until a new influence moved in and quickly made itself felt. Jaffray sensed it immediately, and without stopping to think of possible consequences nailed it down boldly for everyone to see. It was Soviet Russia. A successful revolution had taken place within Russia. The new party, called in those days the Bolsheviks, was in the saddle and riding high. Agents were sent from Russia to China to make what capital they could of the disordered condition.

The propaganda machines were soon turning. China's whole trouble was caused by the imperialism of the Western powers, especially Britain. China was the innocent victim of capitalistic oppression. So ran the propaganda, and it had its effect. "Soon the whole of China—but especially the coastal cities—was all aflame with strong, rapidly spreading antiforeign feeling. As the agitation increased it was concentrated against the British more than any other of the foreign powers, and later it took on an anti-Christian attitude," Jaffray reported in 1926.

Jaffray seldom suspended judgement on any question. Of the Bolsheviks he had no half-way opinion. They were of the devil out and out, he declared, "as wise as the devil, or rather wise with the wisdom of the devil, whose agents they are." They were at bottom anti-Christian, and they

were in China to destroy Christianity there. Of
this Jaffray was sure, and the Bolsheviks themselves had given him his cue. Were they not
rashly boasting in those days that they would
deliver the people from religious superstition and
"pull that bearded god from the skies"?

At first they were content with throwing the
British out of China along with any other stray
foreigners they happened to run across—includ-
ing all missionaries, of course. The inflamed populace took up the manhunt. Soon the circle widened to take in not only all missionaries but all
Christians as well. The church was subjected to a
tornado of persecution. Chinese Christians were
beaten and thrown into prison to be half-starved
and almost frozen. They were ostracized, driven
out and boycotted. In short, all the old tricks of
the enemies of God were used against them to try
to break their faith. As others had done before
them, the Bolsheviks tried to destroy the church
by murdering Christians. This effort has always
failed wherever and whenever it has been tried
through the centuries, but the Bolsheviks did not
know this. In the meantime, the Christians of
China had to endure one more grim experiment.

About the middle of 1925 the British and
American consuls ordered every one of their com-
patriots to leave China proper and proceed to
Hong Kong. This was felt necessary to prevent the
possibility of actual bloodshed. Jaffray advised
his workers to comply with the order. The antiforeign movement would not last long. It was

called by the Chinese a *fung-chiu*—wind and tide—and, reasoned Jaffray, if you wait a little while the wind will die down and the tide will turn.

So to Hong Kong they went and there they stayed until the order came permitting them to return to Wuchow. But hardly had they gotten back and unpacked their bags when a sudden resurgence of antiforeign activities compelled them to leave again posthaste. So it went for many months and years, while Russia, working behind the scenes, put the heat on Britain to dislodge it from China. The missionaries were caught in the cross fire, and though not directly concerned, they were forced to suffer along with those who were.

While compelled to bend somewhat before the storm, Jaffray did not take things lying down. He kept his head, and more than that, he kept before him his well-defined philosophy of Christian missions. He was rarely taken unawares. Whatever the Bolsheviks did he usually was ahead of them, and where he could not anticipate them he could quickly appraise their acts and place them correctly in the order of God's purposes.

The growing unfriendliness toward foreigners he saw as a rough but effective way of divorcing the national church from the foreign missionaries and throwing it back upon God Himself for support. This he conceived to be a distinct blessing, and put down among the "benefits of the present turmoil" an "enforced handing over to the Chi-

nese workers much of the work that had formerly
been in the hands of the foreign missionaries."
This was right in line with his lifelong philosophy
of the indigenous church. He saw the day coming
fast when the foreign missionaries could leave
China to be evangelized by Chinese Christians.
Then the missionaries would be free to push
south in search of other sheep who had not yet
heard the gospel.

He also saw modernism as a real threat to the
gospel in China. Many of the missionaries working under the various boards were modernists.
For the person who was ostensibly Christian but
was secretly an enemy of the faith, Jaffray had
nothing but contempt. He saw many of these people leave the field never to return, and it pleased
him. God had His own way of doing things, undoubtedly.

Never during the four years of turmoil did the
work of Alliance missionaries in South China
come to a stop. Under the most discouraging
handicaps they performed huge amounts of work.
For instance, in 1927 during a lull in active opposition, a campaign of gospel advertising by
means of billboards was carried on throughout all
of China. Never did the *Bible Magazine* suspend
publication nor even miss one issue. The *South
China Tidings*, which went to all of the world and
kept the work before its praying and paying readers, continued to appear. It might be late sometimes, but give Jaffray and his workers a little time

and they were sure to slip past enemy lines to get an issue off the press.

Jaffray himself never stopped writing and at one time mentioned casually how he had been compelled to "write one hundred pages of the *Bible Magazine*" himself for one issue. Gospel literature of every kind continued to flow out from Wuchow to every part of China. The Bible school carried on. The churches never closed their doors. The Christians in China learned to take it. Cast down they might be, but not destroyed.

By 1927 Jaffray had labored in South China more than 30 years, had sparked the advance into French Indochina and for a long time had carried on his heart the burden of both fields. He was now 55, at an age when men generally do not take kindly to major changes in the patterns of their existences. His life had been a success. He had established himself in the esteem of millions in the homeland, had talked familiarly with many of the world's great and was loved by Christians of every denomination throughout the Far East. His own missionary society wanted to honor him.

About this time he received from the International Council of The Christian and Missionary Alliance a cable asking him to become vice president of the Society. To the council he cabled back a polite refusal. To his personal friends he gave the true explanation: "I couldn't come down to that," he said simply.

Years and age and success meant nothing to Jaffray. He was watching the Cloud, not the calendar, and the Cloud was lifting. No one else had noticed it yet, but he thought he saw it moving slightly, and he had seldom been mistaken in the past. Of one thing he was certain: he would follow it whatever direction it took.

15

The Call of
the Islands

FOR A NUMBER OF YEARS JAFFRAY had felt a desire to go toward the south. He had sensed that the Cloud was moving toward the South Seas, but he could not quite get liberty to go. There was an inward block, and he had to wait for it to break up. In the meanwhile he prayed and consulted maps, always searching maps and atlases and any other sources of information he could discover. The offices of the various steamship companies saw him often there, begging maps and chatting with the old salts who had sailed the seas and knew the waters of the East Indies.

Toward the end of 1927 Jaffray felt he had enough information to support the inward urge. There were thousands of Chinese in the port cities of the South Seas, and they were without a gospel witness. And the islands teemed with other people who were as yet untouched by the message of the cross. China could get along without him now. Due to his wise policy of training national workers and encouraging the church to depend upon its own efforts, the work could go on without much help from the foreigners. He began to feel that his work in South China was about ended.

In January, 1928, he left China and sailed from Hong Kong south toward the islands, following the Cloud. He landed at Sandakan, British Borneo, but would not stay there. Some work was being done there by missionaries of another society. "I soon saw that there was no desperate need for another mission entering this part of the field. I wished to hasten on to my goal further south and reach the ports of Dutch Borneo." His maps were paying dividends now. He knew where he was headed at last.

No regular steamers ran between the port of Sandakan and the part of Borneo where he wanted to go. At first he toyed with the idea of hiring a Chinese junk for the trip but soon gave it up for, as he said, "The journey might take two days or two weeks according to the will of the winds." So he haunted the docks on the lookout for something more substantial that might be going his way. We can believe that he did some praying.

"After three days," he said later, "when the Lord would have me leave Sandakan, He had a steamer all ready." A Dutch oil tanker had sailed into port and stopped over on its way to Balikpapan. It was no luxury liner, but it would float, and it was going south. So he applied for passage. His request was flatly denied by the agent. The tanker did not carry passengers. Jaffray went on board and hunted up the captain. He found him to be a good-natured Dutchman who spoke English, but the captain merely confirmed the agent's word. The tanker not only did not carry passengers, but was expressly forbidden by law to do so. And besides, there was no cabin anyway.

The latter fact did not bother Jaffray. He wouldn't need a cabin, he explained, but he *did* need to get to Balik-papan. He would stand up during the trip. Would they grant him at least *standing room?*

The captain's resistance went down before the courage of the missionary. "We'll do better than that," he laughed. "We'll give you a canvas cot on deck, and to avoid the technicalities of the law we'll make you Fourth Officer of the ship."

Jaffray was eager but cautious. "And what are the duties of the Fourth Officer?" he inquired uneasily.

"Oh," replied the captain, "if the other three officers die, you just take over."

Jaffray signed on as Fourth Officer of the SS *Sanbodga.* He paid the captain his passage to Balik-papan and the captain paid him his wages as one of the ship's officers. The cost of his passage was never disclosed, but his wages were one shilling.

Balik-papan turned out to be a city of 21,000 people. Here Jaffray stayed two days, surveying the city. He found a heterogeneous mixture of many races—Malay, Javanese, Boeginese, Chinese, Indians, Arabs and Dyacks. To his oft-repeated question, "Is there anyone here who believes in Jesus Christ?" he received only shrugs or blank stares. He finally discovered one lone Chinese man who claimed to know something about Christianity, but his way of life convinced Jaffray that he was not a true Christian. Beyond this no one knew anything about Christ, nor had anyone ever as much as heard His name mentioned.

Veteran though he was of years of pioneering, the sheer spiritual frigidity of the place crept in on his spirit and pinched his heart like a killing frost. He later wrote:

> While in Balik-papan, deep depression of spirit and a feeling of discouragement, doubt and fear seemed to settle upon my soul. It came upon me like a dark, thick cloud of gloom, and I could not shake it off. Only His light and joy finally dispelled the darkness. It did not last long, but long enough to make me realize that I was on the enemy's territory. Yes, here is a place where the supreme rule of Satan has never been disputed. The Prince of Darkness has never been challenged here.

Deep in his heart he determined that this Prince of Darkness *should* be challenged soon. People of faith and courage would come before long, and they would command the Ruler of Darkness, "Let my people go!" Their voices would carry authority, and the bound would go free.

Many years before this, while he was still a

young man back in Canada, Jaffray had heard a
voice speaking within his heart. It had spoken so
clearly that he knew it was the voice of God: "Depart, and I will send thee far hence unto the gen-
tiles." Now as he traveled south from Balik-papan
he heard the voice again. His commission had
not expired. He must still go on. So on he went,
like Abraham, into the south, stopping nowhere
more than three days, taking such travel accom-
modations as he could find, touching all important places along the way.

Of all the travelers since Cain left home to journey in the land of Nod I suppose none ran up a
list of places with names so strange and romantic
as those visited by Jaffray in search of the lost
sheep of the East Indies—Sandakan, Balik-papan,
Samarinda, Dongala, Pare-Pare, Makassar,
Siagaradia, Bangdang, Batavia and Singapore.
And he was not unaware of the charm of these
curious names. One has only to read his letters to
discover his deep feeling for exotic names and
faraway places. He could get thrilled at the name
of a newly discovered tribe or of some remote city
or river among the thousands of islands in the
Pacific.

"I hear the call," he said, "of great cities like
Makassar and Surabaya. Those names were new
to me. They may be new to you. Now they ring in
my ears all day long and are in my dreams at
night! Makassar! Makassar! Surabaya! Surabaya!
They now represent to me places of midnight
darkness."

On this trip he was quite literally spying out the land. His object was not to preach the gospel so much as to discover where the gospel should be preached. "According to my maps," he reported later, "there are scores of ports on the east coast of Borneo, but as far as we are able to learn there is no Christian witness in any of these places." But there should be soon, he vowed, and he made a few marks on his maps and moved on.

16

Debts and Bloodstains

UPON HIS RETURN TO WUCHOW he dutifully reported to the Board of Directors in New York the results of his exploratory journey in the East Indies and requested permission to open this new field.

More was involved in this request than would appear on the surface. The Society was already extended well beyond its income. Its workers received no guaranteed salaries. The monthly allowances were low at best, pitifully low when compared with the earnings of people in other lines of work. And even this small stipend was contingent upon there being enough on hand at the end of the month to meet the payroll. If funds were below the need, they were prorated among the missionaries and all salaried workers at home. Sometimes this meant little more than half the hoped-for amount. By carefully nursing the funds each month tragedy was averted and the work kept alive, but there was usually not much lying around at the end of the year.

Then came Jaffray's request for a huge apportionment of funds for the support of a new field. The board was willing, but how could they allo-

cate funds they did not possess and had little
reason to hope they would ever get? They were
sorry, they cabled, but there was simply no
money to launch the new venture. It would have
to wait.

Jaffray received this news rather impassively.
He was back at his desk in Wuchow and the pressure of his work there temporarily took his mind
off the islands. He admitted that he was engaging
in a bit of self-congratulation after his adventure
in the South Seas. "I was feeling glad," he said,
"after two months' absence to be home. I felt I
had done my bit. I had obeyed His command to
go. I had made my report to the board, and could
now settle down to ordinary work in Wuchow and
leave others the responsibility of the perishing
souls I had found in the uttermost parts." This
was the natural reaction of someone overworked
and tired. And the refusal of the home board to go
along with his plans did not help any.

But the lives of consecrated people are never
their own. To sit back in selfish composure and
plan the future is never an option to those who
have made the great commitment. They are at the
call of Another, and at any time they may receive
orders to pick up and move on. This is one of the
penalties they must pay for the high privilege of
serving God, and if seen from a low point it looks
like a hard and unsatisfactory way to live. But the
truest appraisal of a way of life is always made at
the end of it. Who that have placed themselves at

the disposal of God and humanity have ever been sorry at the end of life that they did so? Not one, and that is the best argument for the excellence of the devoted life.

Jaffray thought he was resting. He thought he had shifted from his shoulders the burden of the island world. But all the while within him strong forces were secretly working. He had not dismissed the burden—he had only driven it deeper into his heart.

One night as he lay asleep a dream came to him, a dream so vivid and so terrible that he could never doubt its meaning. In telling about it afterward he half apologized. He wanted everyone to know that he had not had many dreams to which he attached special significance. He was not a visionary nor was he much given to the strange and wonderful, but this was different. He was sure it was from God. As he described it:

It was a horrible dream. I thought I was at home. I thought I was a fugitive fleeing from justice, with stains of human blood on my hands. I thought the Lord Jesus was pursuing me. I was full of fear and running for my life. The pure white snow was on the ground. I stopped and tried to wash the bloodstains from my hands in the snow. I looked around and ran again.

I awoke, and my first words were, "Oh, Lord Jesus, what does this mean? I am not running away from Thee. I have no bloodstains on my hands. I am washed clean in Thy precious blood. Oh, teach me what this means."

At once this Scripture came to mind: "Son of man, I have made you a watchman for the house of Israel; so hear the word I speak and give them warning from me. When I say to a wicked man, 'You will surely die,' and you do not warn him or speak out to dissuade him from his evil ways in order to save his life, that wicked man will die for his sin, and I will hold you accountable for his blood."

Jaffray needed no Daniel to interpret this for him. It was all too frightfully plain. He thought at once of the lost of the islands. "If I warn them not, if I preach not the gospel to them, *I will be accountable for their blood*. No wonder I have heard in my ears all these days the cry of the people of Borneo. No wonder I have had ringing in my ears by day and night, 'Balik-papan! Balik-papan! Samarinda! Samarinda!' "

It was a painful and humbling experience as the full meaning of the dream worked itself out into his consciousness. "In my heart I hear a voice saying, 'I have other sheep that are not of this sheep pen. I must bring them also.' And again, 'Whom shall I send? And who will go for us?' " Who would take the gospel to Samarinda and Balik-papan?

"There are Muslim mosques in those places," Jaffray cried. "Idolatrous temples are there. Movie theaters and gambling halls and worse places are there, all in full swing, but in these places there is no Light. Christ has not been named there." He felt himself a debtor to the whole East Indies. As God helped him, he would discharge that debt in full.

As he brooded over this his faith mounted up. "The Light will yet shine in those dark places," he promised himself and God. "Gospel halls will soon be opened for Him there, and His songs will yet be sung by many hearts now deep in sin and in bondage to the devil. The interior of Borneo and the Celebes will someday hear the glad sound of the gospel, and headhunters who live in the jungle will see the great Light and be saved."

Had these words been spoken by anyone lesser than Jaffray, they could have been merely the lyric expression of feeble hope, the beautiful but weak desire of a dreaming soul. Actually they were a true prophecy, an accurate forecast of what would take place within a year of the day they were spoken.

The New York board heard again from Jaffray, and this time it was not a request. It was a declaration. He was going to Borneo. If they could not support him, he would go anyway. God was in this, and God would see him through. Back to Wuchow went a cable giving official permission to enter Borneo under the blessings of The Christian and Missionary Alliance. Where the money would come from was a secret known only to God. There was still no provision for it in the budget.

17

What Is of First Importance?

THE SIGHT OF THE MILLIONS in the East Indies had shaken Jaffray to the center of his being. He had come away determined that they should hear the gospel soon. True, there were multitudes in China who were as yet un-evangelized, but the work of God had gotten a good start there—the church was organized, the major cities had a witness for Christ, and the rest could be reached before long by the normal efforts of the established churches. He felt free now to consider leaving China and moving on to a field that needed him more than China did.

Some time before the dream that decided his relationship to the East Indies enterprise, he had been greatly burdened for the vast number of human beings yet untouched with the gospel. He had, he confessed, been having a deep searching of heart over the whole matter of the church and its responsibility in the world. The question he had been asking, which indeed had been wring-ing his conscience, was this: What is of *first* importance now in light of the world's need and the soon coming of the Lord?

He surveyed the field of Christian endeavor and admitted that he saw the importance of many lines of activity. Deeper-life conferences he felt to be one of the vital needs of China. Believers should be led into the Spirit-filled life. But was that the first? He thought not. Then there was the need for further consolidation of the church. "I have worked hard all my life for the self-supporting indigenous church in China, but in view of the Lord's speedy return, important as the policy of self-support may be, it does not compare with, nor does it conflict with, that which is of *first* importance. I believe in revivals. I am not only praying for this, but confidently believing that in all the world God will graciously revive His work and save many, many souls. But I also believe that souls won from those parts of the earth where as yet no witness has been given are especially precious in His eyes." So his conclusion was, "That which is of *first* importance is the carrying of the message to those who have never heard."

Because he believed that Christ should have in His church representatives from every tribe on earth, he went to the East Indies. Nothing would be easier than to challenge his theological position here, and nothing would be more profitless. If he was in error in believing that God had a special yearning for those who have not heard the gospel, it was an error that brought into being one

of the most fruitful fields in the history of Christian missions.

At first he was not sure just whom God was
going to send to the islands. Someone would go
to them soon—this much he knew by a kind of
spiritual instinct. And, practical as he was, he
noted all the angles. "It will take some sacrifice,"
he said. "It will cost tears and blood. Much
money will be needed. Much hardship must be
endured. Lives will have to be sacrificed for
Christ. But are there not people who will gladly
give of their wealth for such an enterprise? And
are there not young people who will gladly lay
aside all comforts of life and endure hardness as
good soldiers of Jesus Christ, if need be laying
down life itself at His feet?"

Here we are listening to the seer, the man of
vision who knew God's mind and who had an
intimate knowledge of human nature. He knew
these young people would come, and they did
come when the call went out, and they suffered,
and some of them died as he had foretold.

At first he was not sure who would go or
whether he himself should be among them. After
the dream of debts and bloodstains, though, he
was in doubt no longer. He had the answer in his
heart—he must be among the first to go. He must
not ask others to do what he himself would shrink
from doing. That he had already pioneered two
major mission fields did not, as he saw it, relieve
him of his obligation. The debt lay heavy upon
him. "We are debtors to the Chinese, the Malays,

the Javanese, the Indians, the Arabs of these parts, and most of all to the unreached people of the interior. We are accountable for their blood." The burden had followed the Cloud south to the islands. Jaffray now knew himself to be, by divine appointment, a missionary to the East Indies. His heart was there—it only remained for him to wind up his affairs in China and transfer the sphere of his activity to the South Seas.

Now arose the problem of finding missionaries to enter the new field. There were none who could go. He could take none from China. The home board could supply none. Yet somewhere there must be men and women of God's own appointment who were willing to go.

A knowledge of how Jaffray attacked problems of the work may be gleaned from his letters and reports. Those written at this time are especially revealing. He literally soaked his heart in the Word of God. He did not "study" it: he devoured it; he dug himself into it; he transferred its stories and promises to himself and to his work as if the whole Bible had been written for him alone. The great action chapters of the Bible were boldly made to mean *Jaffray* or *Borneo* or *Makassar* or anything else that came into the missionary picture. If Jesus said "other cities", He meant Samarinda and Balik-papan. If He cast a legion of devils out of the maniac of Gadara, He was also waiting to cast devils out of the headhunters of the interior of Borneo and Celebes. If Moses was sent to say to Pharaoh in the name of God, "Let my people go!'' Jaffray was sent no less certain to say the same to the dark rulers of the souls of the East Indies.

This mental habit of making the Scriptures mean some present-day and identifiable person or city or island was a marked feature of the workers who came at Jaffray's call to carry the gospel to the Dutch East Indies. They all caught it from Jaffray. Every danger they faced, every opposition they met, every hardship they suffered could be accounted for by referring to the Word of God. A band of adventurers they were, and of necessity had to be, and it was well for them that they were among the most thoroughly Bible-panoplied Christians that ever went out to battle. They literally used the Scriptures as a sword to cut down the enemy, a hammer to break the rock and a fire to burn through the jungle. Nothing could happen to them that did not have its counterpart in Scripture. They knew themselves to be sent of God as certainly as any prophet or apostle ever did, and their courage was a solemn and wonderful thing to see.

But how to begin—that was Jaffray's burden. From the home office he could expect nothing; he had permission, but nothing more. Then, like a burst of light, the answer came. The first responsibility in the islands was to preach the gospel to the Chinese who swarmed by the thousands through every coastal city. Who could better teach them than Chinese Christians? He would send Chinese as missionaries. He had them by the scores, trained in the Wuchow Bible School. He only had to present his case and he had no doubt that they would respond at once.

A little more thought and another idea was born. He would found a missionary society to work in close cooperation with the Alliance, to be composed altogether of Chinese Christians. This he immediately did, forming the Chinese Foreign Missionary Union. Its birthplace was Hong Kong. Jaffray was from the first its animating spirit, with Pastor L.T. Chao and Leland Wang as two of its most prominent members. It was expected that this new society would draw to it Christians who might be sent as missionaries to the East Indies. A further idea behind it was that it should serve as a normal approach to certain wealthy Chinese who might have funds that they would invest in a Christian project wholly Chinese even though they would look with chilly favor upon any society with a foreign name or origin.

This little society never grew to very large proportions. It did serve as a spark to start off the work in the Indies, but the hope of securing the backing of wealthy Chinese never materialized. The society existed for a few years, mainly on paper, and then expired painlessly and rather obscurely, as it had begun. But it had served a certain end and could die without causing too much embarrassment to anyone. Anyway, Jaffray cared nothing for organizations as such. They must contribute to the cause of world evangelization or they were better dead.

18

The Sound of Marching

WHEN ONCE HIS PLANS WERE CLEARLY out-
lined, the speed with which Jaffray
worked was incredible. By July 1928—
only four months after his return from his first
visit to the islands—he had a Chinese missionary,
Pastor S.W. Chue, hard at work in Makassar. A
few months later Leland Wang was making a
preaching trip among the islands, breaking
ground for the messengers that were to follow.
Exactly one year from the date of his first trip he
again left Wuchow for the island world. This time
he was not alone. With him were two Chinese
Christians, Mr. Lam and Mr. Lin, youthful-look-
ing and half Jaffray's physical size, but filled with
zeal to preach the gospel in the East Indies.

Lam and Lin were left on the east coast of Borneo to open Balik-papan and Samarinda. Jaffray
himself hurried back to Wuchow from where he
issued a ringing call for volunteers to help in the
new work.

The idea caught on. The call was answered from
the homeland. The home board could not help

much, but Jaffray knew where help could be found. The money began to come in. Jaffray did not hesitate to dip into his own private funds to finance the work. Friends in Canada and the United States came to Jaffray's aid. The ball was rolling now and growing larger as it went. Again Jaffray appealed to The Christian and Missionary Alliance, this time not for money but for personnel. In the meantime he worked every legitimate scheme to secure help. He proved to be a master publicist. The words *Borneo, Dyack* and *headhunter* began to be heard throughout Alliance circles and among Christians of other denominations, and the words carried a strange fascination. An unusual type of missionary began to appear asking for assignment to the East Indies. They wanted to serve under Jaffray. The best of them were sent out at once and put at his disposal.

For his headquarters, Jaffray chose the city of Makassar, on the island of Celebes across the strait from Borneo. In less than three months the old familiar *South China Tidings* carried a picture of the new gospel hall in Samarinda, telling its readers that a dream had become reality. They could look at the very building where the gospel was being proclaimed on the island of Borneo. By September a new magazine made its appearance. It was called *The Borneo Pioneer* and was edited by Jaffray and printed in Wuchow on the old Alliance Press. Missionaries began to study the Malay language, and plans got under way for a Bible school and a printing press.

Less than two years after the start of the work, five foreign missionaries had been added to the Chinese workers on the field. Stations had been opened on three important islands of the East Indies group and the *Bible Magazine* was being published in Malay. In addition, a missionary launch had been built in Hong Kong and shipped to Borneo. Now it was chugging up the island's swift rivers carrying the messengers of Christ inland to the Dyacks.

During this period Jaffray still maintained his home in Wuchow, but he was there very little. He spent his time in incessant travel from one end of the East Indies to the other, making what contacts he could with persons who might help him in the work, interviewing Dutch officials and always studying his maps and planning new openings for the gospel. "A new map of the Dutch East Indies from the missionary standpoint has just been issued," he wrote in 1930. "I saw it in the Consul's office. Again my heart was deeply stirred at the sight of the vast unoccupied territories. We have already set our faces toward some of the largest of the unreached fields, but among the tens of thousands of islands of the Dutch East Indies there remains much land to be possessed for the Lord Jesus."

He was now 57 years old, still plagued by diabetes and forced to stay on a sugar-free diet. His heart, though somewhat improved, was still a burden to him. Yet the program he laid out for himself would have challenged the strength of a young and healthy person.

He visited most of the larger islands of the East Indies during those first years, motoring across Java from east to west entering every city of importance on the island. Fabled Bali received a visit from him also, and there he decided a station should be opened at once. The Balinese boasted that there were no Christians on the island, and Jaffray took up the challenge. "There will be," he replied and went to work.

Almost immediately converts were made. The people welcomed the gospel eagerly. Indications pointed to a quick and fruitful harvest on the island.

Bali was the playground of the rich and idle from every part of the world. Its beautiful women, soft breezes and the people's languorous dances were legendary. The yearly take from tourism ran into large figures, and the always-practical Dutch officials were not willing to let anything interfere with this revenue. After stalling for a while, they issued an order forbidding the preaching of the gospel on the island and notified the missionaries that they must desist from holding public meetings of any kind.

This was a blow to Jaffray and the missionaries. The outworking of the order brought the evangelization of the island to a full stop. But if the work could not proceed on Bali, there were scores of other islands where no prohibition existed. Millions of men and women of many races were there waiting for the message, so the missionaries wasted no time lamenting. They simply crossed over the narrow strait and went to work elsewhere. But the seed had been sown, and there were now a few Christians on Bali.

The months that followed were wonderful for the islands. By the end of 1931, 13 foreign missionaries were on the new field. A growing number of Chinese missionaries were working alongside them. Eight stations had been established, a vast amount of exploration had been done, hundreds had been baptized and a real church had come into being in the Dutch East Indies.

Wherever he might be and whatever he might be doing, Jaffray never failed to report back to the Christian public that was making his work possible. From many points along the islands his letters went out to praying friends in every part of the world. And his magazines continued to appear with surprising regularity.

"This is God's day for Borneo, Celebes, Sumatra and many other smaller islands of the Dutch East Indies group," he wrote in 1931. "There is 'the sound of marching tops of the balsam trees.' It is dangerous, even disastrous, to go forth in our own strength, before the Lord's time as indicated by His supernatural sign. But it is even more disastrous to hesitate in unbelief where there is 'the sound of marching' from the Lord."

19

Good-bye to Wuchow

WHILE JAFFRAY WAS STILL CHAIRMAN of the South China field, Alliance missionaries in the Philippines became discouraged with the work there. They decided to close the work and go elsewhere. Jaffray heard about this and at once took command of the situation. From his own field he pulled out some of his badly needed workers and sent them to the Philippines with instructions to do everything in their power to save the work. Several missionaries went, among them Rev. J.A. MacMillan, formerly associate editor of *Alliance Life*, then called *Alliance Weekly*. Their efforts were successful and the work was saved.

The credit for this goes to the missionaries who went to the Philippine islands under difficult conditions. With their optimism and zeal, they turned defeat into victory. Jaffray himself did not go. His part was to see the need and do something about it while there was still time. We do not think of Jaffray in connection with the evangelization of the Philippines. But the simple truth is that if it had not been for him the splendid work done there might never have been accomplished. The hope of the work once rested on him, and he did not fail it.

In writing this story I have one regret—in order to throw into relief the person and work of Jaffray, I am compelled to pass over in comparative silence the lives of numerous men and women who labored with him and without whom he could never have accomplished his mighty deeds. Many of his coworkers were in their own right worthy of a high place in the history of Christian missions. While I am unable to do them justice, I make this rather lame acknowledgement of their spiritual greatness, and take what comfort I can from the knowledge that even the sacred writer, while sketching the life of David, found it necessary to pass over with a mere mention some of David's "mighty men" who would themselves have been rich biographical material.

The evangelization of the South Seas had not been long under way when the great financial crisis of the early 1930s—felt around the world and known through several long, hard years as the Depression—hit the industrialized world. Millions of men were unemployed, and the earning power of the fortunate ones who could work was cut to a fraction. No matter how good the intentions, no one could give to missions money that they did not possess. The consequence of this was greatly decreased income for foreign missions. Boards struggled through some tough years, never knowing what the next month would bring.

Jaffray was in the East Indies when the crash came, but he felt the shock soon enough. Letters began to come from various parts of the world telling of the decline in income among people who had been generous donors to the work. Some may have suggested that Jaffray accept the gloomy economic situation as an indication of God's will for the time and curtail his activities in the islands. For any who felt that way, he had an answer, strictly typical of him: "Do you ask, 'In view of the terrible economic depression of today, do we dare go forward into these new fields and commence new work?' Yea, rather may we ask this—'Dare we, in the face of the command of the Lord Jesus and in the face of the encouraging miracles He is working on our behalf, hesitate for one moment?' "

Here we have Jaffray in essence. It was this habit of getting the Word of God into his projects and then confirming the whole thing by an appeal to divine providences that made him indomitable.

For the first months of his work in the East Indies he maintained his headquarters in Wuchow. His home continued to be the lovely house where he had lived since first coming to China. But Borneo was a long way from Wuchow. Obviously something would have to be done.

By 1931 it became evident that the time had come for the Jaffrays to leave China for good. The migration was not going to be easy. In spite of his world outlook and his constant traveling, Jaffray still loved his home. For 34 years he had lived at

Wuchow, making it his true home. In Wuchow
little Margaret had been born, to win her father's
heart and strike the roots of his affection further
into the earth of China. There in his own familiar
room he had bowed to take kneeling down the
double blow of the deaths of his father and
mother. Wuchow was indeed his home. As often
as he had to leave it, he had come back again with
the homing instinct of the swallow. While he was
away, he always kept his letters pouring in from
wherever he might be.

By this time Margaret was a grown woman. She
had gone through school, first in China and then
in the United States, and had returned to China
as a missionary under the Alliance. The shift of
the family home from Wuchow to the South Seas
did not mean much to her—it was natural for
young people like her to strike out for themselves.

For Mrs. Jaffray the story was different. For all
those years in Wuchow she had been her husband's other self. Her own hands had made the
home that he had loved so solemnly. She too had
roots, and they were in Wuchow as truly as her
husband's were. Now she must prepare to leave it
all just when, with the shadows of approaching
age, she needed it most. But a true gospel trooper
she proved to be. With a smile that she could not
have felt too deeply, she helped her husband
pack their household goods for shipment to
Makassar, on the island of Celebes.

Jaffray had returned to Wuchow to take charge
of packing. The furniture was crated along with

the wedding presents they had treasured for 30 years. Heirlooms and valuable pieces that had been picked up in many out-of-the-way places went into strong boxes for the long journey. Jaffray's books were an item all by themselves, for he had always been an avid reader and a discriminating buyer. His shelves had been lined with thousands of excellent volumes. Into the boxes went the scores of little things that accumulate around a house that has been a true home—things to which human hearts attach a deep and lovely meaning that no unsympathetic outsider can ever understand.

Jaffray smiled and shook off the sadness as he had always done when things were going roughly for him, but there is something touching in his remark, "At last I begin to realize that I am actually leaving Wuchow." He was now 58 years old. For years he had not allowed himself to believe that he would live anywhere else but in Wuchow. Now the trucks were at the door, the goods were carried out and the old place was a home no more.

Mrs. Jaffray took a last look and followed her husband. That was the lot of a missionary wife. It would not have done any good to object. As much as Jaffray loved his wife and his home, he would not allow that love to stop him. Within him was a drive far more powerful than human affection. He belonged to God. By every right of holy vow and solemn covenant he was God's. And he heard the voice of God saying, "Depart and I will

send you unto Pharaoh, and thou shalt say, 'Let
my people go.' " He could do no less than obey.

20

A Vision Fulfilled

IN ATTEMPTING TO OUTLINE THE WORK of Alliance missions during those first fruitful years in the Dutch East Indies, one is forced to select, rejecting material so abundant and wonder-filled as to seem positively incredible. As Jaffray said of it, "It was truly apostolical."

The personnel of the Alliance in the East Indies was never very large. The actual roster of missionaries never exceeded 30, the Chinese workers numbered 20 and the native workers peached 140. That was in 1941. The amazing work of the preceding 10 years was accomplished by a far smaller corps of workers scattered through the East Indies from Djambi, Sumatra to New Guinea and from Long-Berang, Borneo south to the island of Lombok.

I have tried throughout this book to avoid trying to account for things. I have simply tried to set down the facts and let the reader furnish his or her own explanation. That I have not always adhered to my purpose I readily admit. And now the temptation to try to understand the success of the work in the East Indies is too strong to be resisted. When a historian turns philosopher he or she often goes astray, but I venture a few remarks nevertheless.

The first thing I noticed about the East Indies project that would seem to explain its success was that the call of God was remarkably clear. God Himself had moved ahead of Jaffray into the islands. The work *had* to succeed. Another reason for the success was the type of missionary sent to work with Jaffray. There seemed to be hardly an ordinary one on the field. Each one was marked by some special gift, some extraordinary ability, and the whole band taken together constituted just about the most wonderful army of men and women ever engaged in the work of foreign missions. For brooding mysticism, for adventurous courage, for slashing enthusiasm, for high spiritual determination—their equal would be hard to find.

The weight of the spiritual burden carried by these men and women might also account for the power that attended their labors. An example of this was the tremendous prayer of Jaffray himself. Only the Biblical expression "groanings that cannot be uttered" can fully express the intensity of his praying. And the efforts of such prayers were often startling.

One year while Jaffray and Rev. Gustave Woerner were traveling in Borneo visiting newly opened stations, they came to Kalosi, which up to that time had been marked by a strange unresponsiveness to the gospel. It was as if an invisible ring had been drawn around the place and the people living inside the circle had been struck deaf and dumb. However the truth might prevail everywhere else, not one convert could be made inside that circle. In addition to a total apathy toward the gospel, there was among the people an active hostility wholly foreign to the rest of the island. Here the two missionaries stayed overnight.

Jaffray lay down at the usual time to sleep, apparently in normal health. In the middle of the night, Woerner was suddenly awakened by the sounds of a commotion in the room where Jaffray slept. He rushed into the room and found Jaffray struggling and groaning in agony. All his motions were those of a man wrestling with someone trying to choke him to death, an invisible antagonist who seemed about to kill him. This continued for a short time and then suddenly ceased. Immediately Jaffray came to consciousness weak and badly shaken. Woerner prayed with him and ministered to him as he was able, and Jaffray's strength returned slowly. By morning he was feeling well again.

The struggle of the night before he never doubted was a personal engagement with the devil himself. He stated boldly that he had met and in prayer had conquered the "prince" who had been responsible for the strange bondage of the people in and around Kalosi. By quick accommodation of Scripture to his needs, he saw in this "prince" Pharaoh who was holding the people in bondage. Jaffray sternly commanded him to "let my people go!" He had no doubt that the prince had been routed and the way opened for the deliverance of the people from the bondage. Were we to stop here the whole thing might be smiled off tolerantly as the pardonable weakness of an intensely religious man, and nothing more. But there is a significant sequel. Almost at once the whole situation changed within that previously barren circle. The indifference of the people melted like ice before the summer sun. The work of conversion that was sweeping across Borneo broke out at Kalosi and the men of the district began to turn to Christ in large numbers. The gospel began to triumph. From that time on there was great fruit and the opposition ceased.

Makassar was the hum of all the varied activities in the islands. There a Bible school and a printing press were established, following the pattern in Wuchow and Hanoi. The old Alliance Press, which had seen such worthy service in Wuchow and which Jaffray was planning to move to Makassar, was suddenly destroyed one night in the fall of 1932. With no motive that anyone could discover, a mysterious person slipped in while no one was on watch and burned the whole thing to the ground. Nothing was left but the crumbling walls. Machinery, paper, stock, type—everything was a total loss.

This brought to an end the plan to move the press to Makassar. Something else had to be done, and it was accomplished with little loss of time. Through generous use of his own funds and the gifts of faithful friends, new presses were secured and set up in Makassar. Jaffray's *Bible Magazine*, under another name, soon made its appearance. Hymn books, tracts, commentaries and devotional literature soon began to roll off the presses in a constantly growing stream.

But most important of all was the success of the work in the number of converts. Considering the type of men and women found in the islands, this is all the more remarkable. In Borneo, for instance, the people were headhunters chained to a thousand superstitions and without written language.

Within five years from his first visit to the East Indies Jaffray could write in his annual report: "What a wonderful year 1934 has been in the short history of the Alliance work in the Netherlands East Indies. No less than 4,347 souls have accepted the Lord Jesus, have hurled their idols and fetishes to the bats and have confessed their new Master in baptism. They are coming quickly and in large numbers."

The report for 1934 was so typical of Jaffray that a long look into his heart could be taken by reading it. Under the title "Lengthening and Strengthening" he made his report to the home board and the conference and the Christian public who had supported him. Along with this accounting went a terrific appeal to his own workers to pour into their work their last ounce of strength. "Lengthen thy cords to the uttermost parts of the earth. This is the true spirit of pioneer missionary enthusiasm. Lengthen thy cords! Enlarge! Spread out! Break forth!"

"And this," he says crisply, speaking again to the outside world, "is what we have been trying to do here in the East Indies for the last five years. We have not busied ourselves treading on the toes of other missionaries. We have sought only new fields, virgin soil, untouched regions where Christ has not been named. God has been with us and by His help we have entered at least 10 new fields where there was no gospel witness before we came."

True to the old pattern shown him at the first, he was not satisfied merely to advance. "We must strengthen as well as lengthen," he said. "These two phases of missionary work go hand in hand—the lengthening first and then the strengthening. And how can this be done? The Word of God is our foundation. Therefore the teaching of the Word faithfully, systematically and thoroughly to the students in our Bible schools—the education of a native ministry thoroughly grounded in the Word of God—is of first importance."

By 1941 his statistical report was astounding. One hundred thirty-nine gospel centers had already been opened. The Makassar Bible Institute had an enrollment of 209 that year. There were 74 Sunday schools with 3,200 students attending; 13 primary schools with an enrollment of 479; and 11,094 converts duly accepted into the church. The church's income reached 11,323 guilders.

Another project that engaged Jaffray's attention

during those days was the opening of a mission in British Malaya. As I have repeatedly pointed out, Jaffray was an explorer. But he differed from Ponce de Leon or Amundsen in that he was not primarily interested in geography but in people. He went out not to look for rivers but for men and women, as a shepherd in the story went out to search for the sheep that was lost.

Jaffray's Malaya project was one of the few that did not meet with much success. It had looked good as he had figured it. From the southern tip of British Malaya a narrow chain of mountains ran roughly northward, following the peninsula up to the mainland and on through Burma to the border of West China. In these mountains, according to Jaffray, there lived scores of unknown tribes—with a total population of thousands— who had never heard the gospel. His plan was to open a church in Malaya, establish a strong church there, found a Bible school and use this as a base of operation to work up the mountain range into China. To carry out this work he planned to use mainly Chinese Christians, along with the indigenous people who might accept the faith and prepare themselves for the task.

The plan was not too well taken by the other missionaries of the East Indies. They either did not see it or they felt it to be premature. Jaffray, however, was not discouraged by their indifference. He set bravely to work to bring his plan to fruition.

Back in Canada a short time before this, the old

Toronto *Globe* had been sold and a generous amount of cash had come to the Jaffray family from the sale. This put at Jaffray's disposal extra funds, as he saw it, for such a time as this. To carry out his plans he did not hesitate to draw upon these funds heavily. The site chosen for the Malay work was Ringlet, Cameron Highlands, about 300 miles north of Singapore. There on a 10-acre plot of ground a mission station, a Bible school and a missionary rest home were built at a cost of 18,000 Singapore dollars. The cost of this was borne almost entirely by Jaffray himself.

The Christian and Missionary Alliance was never much interested in this project, and very little help could be expected from the missionaries of the East Indies. Jaffray was pretty much alone. He did, however, have one loyal disciple who would have followed him over a cliff if he commanded it. This was Gustave Woerner. Jaffray sent him to Ringlet and made him general head of the new station. The Worldwide Christian Couriers, headed by Paul Rader, gave some assistance. Some fruit attended the work, and with the Jaffray funds behind it, the whole thing looked promising indeed.

Just how far this would have gone, or how much permanent success would have attended it will never be know. The work was soon brought to a sudden halt by the victorious sweep of the Japanese forces and the fall of Singapore. Jaffray's high hopes for the forgotten people of the mountains ended a few years later in a Japanese prison camp. To this time no one of like vision has come forward to take up the work where the missionary martyr laid it down.

21

The Storm Breaks

R.A. JAFFRAY SPRANG FROM SUPERIOR STOCK. He never forgot that, and he never allowed the other members of his family to forget that he knew and appreciated it. However far they might be separated from each other, each anniversary was duly marked and some token of remembrance, though it often had to be sent halfway around the earth. Letters between the members of the family were frequent and long and filled to the edge with the warmest expressions of love.

In addition to his many letters, Jaffray also managed to see his people in person at fairly frequent intervals, returning home for brief visits every three or four years. His reasons for doing so were several. His health required a good deal of nursing, and a few weeks occasionally in the bracing climate of Canada did much for him both physically and mentally. For many years he was also a member of the board of directors of the Toronto *Globe* and he liked to attend their meetings whenever he could. But the big reason for these visits was his burning desire to meet people who could share his vision and his burden for the world.

124

His last visit was made in 1938. With his wife he journeyed via England to Canada and the United States. While at home he was suddenly taken with an intestinal ailment so serious that the doctor urged an immediate operation if his life was to be saved. This Jaffray refused to consider. He believed that the Lord would deliver him in His own time without recourse to the surgeon's knife. At the urgent advice of the doctor, Will Jaffray sought to persuade his brother to submit to an operation. Still he refused, requesting only a night of privacy in which he might lay the matter before God in prayer. The family waited through the night, not knowing what to expect. As the morning broke he walked out free from pain and apparently well. The ailment did not recur.

For some years Wheaton College had been trying to catch Jaffray at home long enough to confer upon him what they considered to be the well-earned degree of doctor of divinity. The opportunity came during this visit, and he went to Wheaton to receive the degree. As the stately academic procession moved along to the strains of solemn music, he happened to see in the assembly his brother Will who had—unknown to him—driven down from Toronto to be present for the event. Wholly forgetting the dignity of the occasion, he hurried impulsively to his brother's side. After greeting him warmly, he resumed his place in line amid the smiles of the assembled audience. This may be a trifle, but it is altogether characteristic of Jaffray. With him blood was definitely thicker than water. What is mere formality when a man wants to shake hands with his own brother?

World conditions at that time were so threatening as to cause him great concern. While he conceived his ministry to be exclusively spiritual, he was yet remarkably well informed on world events, alert and extremely sensitive to political developments everywhere. The whole international picture he saw in relation to world missions. The Sino-Japanese conflict was then raging, and of course Jaffray was strongly pro-Chinese. He was not, however, concerned with China as a nation—he was thinking of China as a mission field.

During that last visit Jaffray talked freely of his fears for the world. That there would be another world war he had not the slightest doubt, and he knew that this time Japan would be in it. Well-intentioned friends urged him to stay at home, at least for a while, but he would not consider this for a moment. "If I do not go back now," he said, "there is little likelihood that I can ever go back at all. I must return to the Far East. I want to die out there where my life has been."

In the fall of that year he and his wife returned to Makassar. The work went on with increasing tempo. New missionaries began to arrive on the field, the Bible school grew in size and effectiveness and the gospel was carried as far as Wissel Lakes in New Guinea. To cut the time to travel inland from weeks to hours, a new seaplane was purchased and put into use among the islands.

With the declaration of war in Europe in 1939, there came a sharp falling off in missionary funds. A strange sense of impending danger began to be felt among the missionaries, a premonition of troubles and perils ahead. Sensitive to all the flowing currents of his time, Jaffray felt this keenly. He *sensed* rather than saw a coming conquest of the islands by forces hostile to the cross, and the prophet in him took up the challenge.

"God is working with us," he wrote. "If the enemy will not let the people go, God will manifest His wrath and show His great power. It is not easy. It is warfare. Satan reluctantly releases his grip upon his slaves. But eventually he *must* let the people go. Though Pharaoh hardened his heart, boastfully and proudly saying, 'I will not let you go,' yet God said that eventually he *would* let them go." Here he struck back at the foe and defied the power he felt closing in upon him.

He was tired now and one could almost feel the weariness in his words as he sought to console his own heart and strengthen the hands of his workers. Things looked bad, and they would get worse, but whatever came they were to remember that God was with them. This He had proved again and again in the short-but-colorful history of the Alliance in the islands. And they had already seen Him work as He had for Moses in Egypt.

"God is working with us," he told his people. "To those who believe—and thousands are believing—there is redeeming power and deliverance only faintly foreshadowed in the exodus from Egypt. What a joy it will be when we shall meet face-to-face those liberated slaves, a people taken out of all the tribes of the earth for the glory of His name. No sacrifice that we have made will then seem too great. So until He comes, let us go forth to every tribe and people who have not yet heard the gospel, saying, 'Let my people go!' "

It was not long after this that the great storm broke over the Far East and swept down with devastating fury upon the islands of the South Seas. On December 7, 1941, the Japanese—without warning—attacked the American naval base at Pearl Harbor, inflicting upon the U.S. Navy the most crushing defeat in naval history. From there they went wild over the Pacific. Hong Kong was quickly captured, Manila fell, Singapore surrendered and the victorious Japanese forces moved into the Netherlands East Indies on their drive southward toward Australia.

The missionaries were caught in the middle of all this. With a heart for the safety of his workers, Jaffray immediately issued blanket permission for all who desired to leave their posts and proceed to the United States. A few fled the islands. Most of them stayed. Jaffray himself stayed with his workers. "I cannot leave," he said, "while one missionary remains on the field."

In the fall of 1941, Jaffray became so exhausted that a rest seemed imperative. Consequently he—with his wife and daughter, Margaret—left Makassar for a vacation at Baguio, in the Philippines. After a few weeks there he felt better and was impressed that they should return to Makassar. With considerable difficulty they managed to get back again to Makassar, arriving there December 6. When the war broke in the Pacific the next day, Jaffray rejoiced at the evident guidance of God. "He led us," he said, "and brought us to Makassar in His own will and time. We thank God and take courage for the days to come." Nothing that occurred subsequently ever shook his conviction that the Lord Himself was going before him.

22

Labor Ended

THE FIRST FEW MONTHS after the Japanese came to the islands were relatively quiet for the missionaries. A few had managed to escape to the United States. The rest tried to carry on as usual, never knowing, however, just what would happen next. They knew only that they were now enemy aliens a long way from home and that they might expect little mercy from the arrogant and swaggering Japanese soldiers.

Trouble first started in Borneo. Rev. F.C. Jackson, a new missionary and pilot of the mission plane, had given valuable assistance to the Dutch forces when the Japanese had been trying to land on the coast of Borneo. He and his plane had become—for a short time—almost an arm of the Dutch military, and the Japanese did not forget it. Jackson was captured and executed. Another Alliance missionary, Rev. Andrew Sande, died with him. This was the beginning of a series of heavy losses such as few missionary societies, fortunately, have ever been called upon to bear. Within one month Mrs. Sande and her infant son were also killed. Before the terror had run its course, Rev. John Willfinger had been put to death; Rev.

C.R. Deibler had died of neglect; Rev. W.E. Presswood, weakened by overwork, had died of pneu-
monia; and Grace Dittmar, as a result of exposure
on board ship, had died shortly after her return to
the United States.

These had been Jaffray's fellow workers. They
had come to the islands to labor under his direction. For them he had prayed long and often. To
him they had looked for inspiration and guidance. For their sakes he had stayed on in the East
Indies when the stormy wind and tempest was
threatening to break upon them. Is there not a
kind of solemn beauty in the thought that he and
they would lay down their burdens together, that
he would not need to take up the task again after
they had gone from him?

Just before the Japanese arrived in Celebes, Jaffray moved his entire Makassar mission staff to
Benteng Tinggi, a health resort some miles away.
There they carried on what activities their restricted movements would allow. Jaffray did all
possible to sustain the courage of all the Alliance
missionaries in the islands, keeping in as close
touch with them as possible under the circumstances.

The party remained in Benteng Tinggi undis-
turbed until March 13, 1942. Then the Japanese
arrested the men and interned them in huge
police barracks in Makassar. The women were interned in Benteng Tinggi. For reasons that may
never be known, Jaffray was permitted to stay
with his wife and daughter in the women's prison.

It would be an interesting experience to be allowed to look into the mind of the Japanese officer who made the strange decision to hold one man in the women's internment camp. Was it respect for Jaffray's white hair or was there perhaps some quality about the dignified and saintly veteran that moved the soldier's heart to pity? Whatever the reason, Jaffray remained with his family for one year, enjoying perfect privacy, carrying on his literary work as usual.

But this was too good to last. At the end of a year the Japanese took him from his family and placed him in another camp in Molino, Celebes, where he stayed for four months. He was then moved to the men's camp at Pare-Pare. Soon the Allied planes came over and subjected the camp to a terrific bombing. Many were killed. Jaffray himself escaped by only a narrow margin.

After the Pare-Pare camp had been bombed, the prisoners were taken to another camp a few miles further into the mountains and were shut in buildings originally intended for swine. Here Jaffray spent all but the last few of his remaining days on earth.

Rev. W.E. Presswood, who was with Jaffray, described conditions:

> Shortly after our arrival there, dysentery broke out, and in the next three months more than two-thirds of the 600 men took sick with the disease. Of this number, over 25 died. Food was short; sanitary conditions were beyond

description. In the midst of the dysentery epidemic we had constant air raid alarms. American planes flew over and around the camp daily, bombing and machine-gunning in the neighborhood. It was the rainy season and the tropical downpour converted the small creek into a mighty raging torrent during the night.

Our camp life up to this time had been characterized by periods of terrorism by the guards, when men were beaten senseless for the least offense, revived by a pail of water thrown over them, and then beaten again.

This was still not all. Later the prisoners were moved to a place still worse. "Here," wrote Presswood, "our food consisted of a half pound of white rice per day, with nothing to eat along with it. This proved too much for Dr. Jaffray. He weakened rapidly, like everyone else, but because of his age he could not hold out as long."

Very weak now, but smiling and cheerful as always, Jaffray laid down for his final rest. It is a solemn and awful thought that this man whom the continents and islands of the earth could not contain was now contracted to the pitiful and narrow confines of a wretched Japanese prison cot, dying of starvation. Our human hearts would cry against this mighty moral incongruity, this huge injustice and fracture of the moral foundations of mankind. His entire life had been lived for others. He had spent his years searching for the poor of the earth, for the oppressed and enslaved, crying to their oppressors, "Let my people go!" Then he died a victim of the mad hate and lust for power against which he had preached while strength remained in him.

In this picture of the saint dying of exhaustion while evil men spread themselves and, for a little while, throw their weight around, we have in miniature the sad history of the world. Any rebellious thought we might be tempted to entertain is quickly dispelled by the knowledge that when God wanted to save people from their moral suicide, He had to be born in a manger and die on a cross. Jaffray was the willing servant of a God such as this. Under what more fitting conditions, then, could he die, a man who believed as he believed and loved as he loved? He would not have had it otherwise. He *chose* to die in the East Indies.

Dr. R.A. Jaffray died on the night of July 29, 1945. Beside him on the next cot, and himself ill with dysentery, lay Rev. F.R. Whetzel, a missionary of the Batjan Immanuel Mission. He was the last person to see Dr. Jaffray alive and the last one to whom he spoke on earth. Mr. Whetzel writes, "One of the great blessings of my life was the privilege I had of being interned with Dr. Jaffray on the island Celebes. I learned to love him as a great man of vision and faith."

This seems to be the consensus of all who knew this remarkable man. It was a privilege to know him, even if one had to enter a Japanese prison camp to meet him.

Robert Jaffray has left us. His name appears no more on the roster of Alliance missionaries. His challenging voice is heard no more where people gather to plan the evangelization of the world and the bringing back of the King. But his work remains. On three of the great mission fields of the world the church stands as a monument to his love, his faith and his consecration. His days ended under conditions that might, when viewed only from the outside, appear tragic. But not so— in a little lyric outburst written only four years before his death, he gave us the inside picture:

> One day it will all be finished, and the weary feet, all scarred and bleeding, will cross the last mountain, tread the last trail, reach the last tribe and win the last soul. Then He Himself will exclaim, 'Well done, good and faithful servant.' Let us keep our eyes steadily upon the goal. For when we hear the shout from the skies, all else will fade into utter insignificance. Ere long the Lord will descend from heaven with a shout. Even so, come, Lord Jesus.

- If you were inspired by reading *Let My People Go*, why not give copies to your friends? Additional copies are available from Christian Publications by calling toll-free 1-8...

F

-

Name _____

Address _____

City _____ State ____ Zip _____

RJ1